Politics
and Urban
Policies

The Bobbs-Merrill Policy Analysis Series

Politics and Urban Policies

Brett W. Hawkins

THE BOBBS-MERRILL COMPANY, INC.
Indianapolis • New York

JS
422
.H34

James A. Robinson
CONSULTING EDITOR IN POLITICAL SCIENCE

Thomas R. Dye
GENERAL EDITOR, *The Bobbs-Merrill Policy Analysis Series*

Copyright © 1971 by The Bobbs-Merrill Company, Inc.
Printed in the United States of America
Library of Congress Catalog Card Number 77-151612
ISBN-0-672-61060-4 (pbk)
ISBN-0-672-51474-5
Second Printing

Foreword

The aim of the Policy Analysis Series is the systematic explanation of the content of public policy. The focus of the Series is on public-policy choices of national, state, and local governments, and the forces that operate to shape policy decisions.

Books in the Policy Analysis Series are not concerned with what policies governments *ought* to pursue, but rather with *why* governments pursue the policies that they do. Public policies are not debated or argued in these volumes, rather they are assembled, described, and explained in a systematic fashion.

Each volume deals with an important area of public policy—education, taxing and spending, economic opportunity, agriculture, urban problems, military affairs. Each volume treats public policy as an output of political systems and endeavors to explain policy outputs with reference to historical, environmental, political, and cultural forces that generate demands upon political systems. Each volume attempts to employ systematic comparative analysis in the explanation of public policy. This involves the comparison of policies past and present; the comparison of policies generated by national, state, and local political systems; and the comparison of the effects of political, environmental, and cultural forces in the shaping of public policy. Each volume strives for improved theoretical statements about public-policy determination.

Thomas R. Dye

Preface

Politics and Urban Policies is a systematic explanation of what cities do and why they do it. This book is not a polemic on "the urban crisis"; policies are not attacked, defended, or evaluated. Instead, municipal policies are treated as dependent variables, and Brett W. Hawkins systematically explores the urban environmental conditions, political forces, governmental arrangements, and extracommunity influences, that operate to shape these policies.

Systems theory provides the framework for analysis. The book is organized around the important linkages suggested by systems theory—the linkage between the community environment and its political system (Chapter 2), the linkage between the community environment and municipal policy (Chapter 3), the linkage between the community political system and municipal policy (Chapter 4), and finally, the impact of extracommunity influences on municipal policy (Chapter 5).

Reliance is placed upon comparative analysis rather than upon case studies. This book is not a study of New Haven, Connecticut, or Oberlin, Ohio, or Atlanta, Georgia, or New York City. Instead, Professor Hawkins relies upon studies which test explanations of urban policy against the data derived from many cities. The purpose is to develop generalizations about urban policy, not to record what happened in one city.

Professor Hawkins skillfully integrates the existing research literature on city policy with important original research findings to provide a comprehensive and insightful review of urban policy analysis. A wide variety of municipal policies are examined—from water fluoridation, urban renewal, and land use control to annexation, school desegregation, and metropolitan consolidation. Many aspects of community environment are examined—size, income, racial composition, economic base, property value, religious affiliations, and so on. City political systems are described in terms of the structure of government, the partisan or nonpartisan character of elections, the type of electoral constituencies, the extent of metropolitan governmental consolidation, and even the nature of the communities' political elite. Extracommunity influences include political ties with higher levels of government and social-economic ties with private organizations.

Politics and Urban Policies provides us with a summary and critique of the systematic research on city policy. It explores the strengths and weaknesses of systems theory in the explanation of public policy. It is encouraging to see how far the study of local government has progressed since the case study and reform literature of a few years ago. Yet the task of policy explanation has only begun. This volume provides convincing evidence that the systematic, comparative approach to the study of municipal policy can contribute significantly to our general understanding of the causes and consequences of public policy.

Thomas R. Dye
Florida State University

Contents

	List of Tables	x
	List of Figures	xii
1	Politics and Urban Policies: An Introduction	3
2	The Environmental Base of Urban Governmental Forms	19
3	Community Environment and Urban Policies	61
4	Community Politics and Urban Policies	85
5	Extracommunity Influences on Urban Policies	101
6	In Perspective	113
	Index	121

Tables

1–1 Examples of Variables in Figure 1–2 15
2–1 Form of Government in 1933, 1940, 1950, and 1960 by the Percentage of Foreign-Born Persons in 1930, 1940, 1950, and 1960, Respectively 22
2–2 Cramer's V for the Relationship Between the Percentage of Foreign-Born Persons and Governmental Form with and without Control Variables, for the Years 1933, 1940, 1950, and 1960 24
2–3 Forms of Suburban Government by Size and Regional Location 34
2–4 Form of Government by Mobility and Population Change 36
2–5 Form of Government by Proportion in White Collar Occupations and Mobility 37
2–6 Manufacturing Levels, Religious Composition, and Urban Electoral Systems: Competitive States Only 39
2–7 Conditions Associated with Metropolitan Governmental Fragmentation 46

List of Tables

3–1	Correlations and Path Coefficients for the Dependent Variable: Urban Renewal Expenditures	67
3–2	Correlations and Path Coefficients for the Dependent Variable: General Budget Expenditures	68
3–3	The Social Character of Cities and Educational Policy Outcomes	69
3–4	Environmental Variables and Public School Segregation in Northern and Southern Cities	75
3–5	Correlations Between Ethnicity and Religious Heterogeneity and Outputs in Reformed and Unreformed Cities	82
4–1	Correlations Between Selected Independent Variables and Output Variables by Four Categories of Reformism	95
4–2	Metropolitan Governmental Fragmentation and Spending for Services	96
4–3	Metropolitan Governmental Fragmentation, Metropolitan Environment, and Spending for Services	97
5–1	Absentee Ownership and Community Power Structure	111

Figures

1–1	A Political System, Its Environment and Output	12
1–2	Relationships and Variables in Urban Policy Research	14
2–1	Governmental Form and Economic Base: Incidence of Three Systems in Different Types of Cities	31
2–2	Governmental Form and Community Size	33
6–1	Summary Models Ranked According to Explanatory Importance	115

Politics
and Urban
Policies

chapter 1
Politics and Urban Policies: An Introduction

Urban problems are among the most widely discussed phenomena in American life. The reading public is constantly bombarded with terms like "community power structure," "the culture of poverty," "racial schism," and "metro government." These terms, which provoke controversy even among scholars, must surely convey a bewildering variety of images to laymen who stumble across them in magazines and newspapers. One hopes, however, that their persistent appearance will help to develop the layman's interest in urban conflicts and policies, for his interest will be increasingly important to the future of our society.

City life is alternately acclaimed and condemned in the current literature. Some commentators praise the city as a haven for culture, learning, high living standards, technical innovation, and economic power; others excoriate it as a breeding ground for crime, penury, promiscuity, and group conflict.

Many American intellectuals have shown a profound dislike for cities. In fact, a recent essay on antiurbanism concludes that "dismay and distrust have been the predominant attitudes of the American intellectual toward the American city."[1] The essay further suggests that

---

[1] Morton White, "The Philosopher and the Metropolis in American Life," in

the source of this pervasive distrust has not been solely "roughneck prejudice, ignorance, or philistinism." Thomas Jefferson, Ralph Waldo Emerson, Henry David Thoreau, John Dewey, Josiah Royce, and George Santayana have all been prominent figures in the ranks of the antiurbanists.[2] Philosophical antiurbanism still pervades American life and is reflected in efforts to recapture the atmosphere of rural, small-town America in today's suburbs.[3] Its popularity may also help to explain the strident opposition that policy proposals favoring the city often encounter.[4] Conversely, the adoption of pro-city policies may be partially attributable to the less prevalent view that, far from representing the devil's handiwork, the city in fact represents the heartbeat of American civilization. Of course, few analysts would be content to explain urban policies solely in terms of the pro- or anti-city philosophies of voters and officials, much less those of philosophers and essayists. Most observers, thankfully, would argue that other factors are involved.

The main purpose of this book is to summarize what is currently known about the determination of urban policies. This purpose differentiates the present work from most books on urban affairs. The latter are usually concerned with how to go about solving urban problems; their focus, in other words, is on *reform* (in accordance with specified values). *Politics and Urban Policies*, in contrast, focuses exclusively on what *is*, not what might be. The conclusions in this book are based on painstaking research by political scientists, economists, and sociologists, but they reflect as well my own thinking about the current state of urban policy research. For the most part I have tried to put a generous interpretation on research publications in terms of the various authors' intentions and the bearing of their findings on important em-

---

Urban Life and Form, ed. Werner Z. Hirsch (New York: Holt, Rinehart & Winston, 1963), p. 81.

[2] *Ibid.*, p. 82.

[3] See Robert C. Wood, *Suburbia: Its People and Their Politics* (Boston: Houghton Mifflin, 1958).

[4] For a discussion and various papers treating the theme that antiurbanism has inhibited man's ability to cope with urban problems, see Jeffrey K. Hadden, Louis H. Masotti, and Calvin J. Larson, *Metropolis in Crisis* (Itasca, Ill.: Peacock, 1967), Part III.

pirical theories. Less effort has been devoted to criticizing research publications. However, critical comments do occasionally appear throughout the text, and major problems confronting the researcher are discussed in the final chapter. Existing urban policies are neither attacked, advocated, nor otherwise evaluated. Instead, the emphasis is on providing research-based answers to such questions as these:

1. What characteristics differentiate cities that have adopted fluoridation, urban renewal, a city-manager form of government, and metropolitan government from other cities?
2. What characteristics of the urban environment are associated with public spending for welfare and education?
3. What forces from outside the city (extracommunity variables) shape its policies?

In answering these and other questions I assume (as do researchers generally) that when certain factors closely coincide with specified policies those factors help to explain the policies[5]—at least until new research indicates otherwise. Wherever we detect associations we should also develop explanations, though these may be speculative and tentative in nature. In this literature it often happens that to confirm explanations fully would require somewhat different data and measures than those available.

We place special emphasis in this book on comparative studies. Those covering numerous cities (extensive comparative analyses) we rank first in scientific importance because they yield generalizations about *many* cities. After all, studies that associate policy differences among many cities with other intercity differences set forth findings that have greater credibility and wider applicability than studies of only one or a few cities. They tell us what is generally true and permit us to assess influences that in the analysis of one city (or a few) might remain undetected for lack of variation in key variables. What political scientists often try to explain, of course, are differences that they observe between various communities or (less frequently) within the same community over time. Most characteristics of cities vary less in 2 cities than in 51; similarly, they normally vary less in 51 cities than

---

[5] See Thomas R. Dye, *Politics in States and Communities* (Englewood Cliffs, N.J.: Prentice-Hall, 1969), p. 8.

in 212. We rank studies concentrating on a few cities (intensive comparative analyses) second in scientific importance and single-city (case) studies last.

A Review of the Urban Politics Literature: From Good Government, to Who Governs, to Policy Explanation

The study of urban politics from the 1920s through the 1940s consisted mostly of prescribing reformed governmental institutions designed to promote the good of the whole community, describing structural arrangements, and calling for the elimination of group conflict and partisan politics from government. Political scientists acted out the role of a social engineer applying good government, middle class norms to urban ills. Their writings stressed efficiency in the provision of public services, neglected government's role in resolving political and social conflict, and called upon politicians to stop exploiting religious, racial, ethnic, and class differences in the community. By describing formal institutions and the way the laws say they function, scholars left an impression of harmonious, legitimate functioning. The vision of a city free of political conflict appealed to idealists disenchanted with "boss rule" and to all people who found group conflict distasteful. Associated with this feeling was a belief among some people that there is a definable "right" answer to every public question, thus implying that conflict is unnecessary and that differences of opinion are not wholly legitimate. Typically, these persons also believed that the pursuit of "special interests" is immoral, that all men should devote themselves to the "public interest," that there are no fundamental group differences, and that reasonable men can arrive at a "proper" solution through calm deliberation.

However, the good government approach to the study of urban politics was more than a set of middle class norms. It was more than a plan to make urban governments more efficient by banishing politics and adopting nonpartisan elections, civil service coverage, municipal home rule, short ballots, city managers, small councils, and at-large elections. Implicit in the good government movement was the assumption that *formal political power had the potential to control the quality of city life.* The reformers attributed great power to formal government[6] while making little or no effort to compare the impact of formal power with informal power outside of government. They blamed improper governmental forms and structures for such problems as machine-dominated electorates, inadequate public services, and inefficient administrations. Rather than trying to determine the impact of formal political institutions compared with other factors, the reformers assumed institutions to be of critical importance. Significantly, they attempted virtually no systematic comparison of urban governments to see if their own goals were being achieved.

In the postwar period, however, the old formulas began to be questioned. Urban political analysis grew less normative and became more scientific. Several factors accounted for this change. For one thing, reformers themselves became interested in understanding the exercise of power in cities. All too often they found the status quo resistant to reformist efforts. They therefore wanted to know where the real centers of power lay, in order to improve the chances of achieving their reforms. Political scientists also shifted directions. They became interested in analysis of the city as a microcosm of other, larger, political systems. They found the city a convenient locus for research dealing not specifically with the city but with political phenomena that could be conveniently studied in an urban setting—phenomena such as voting behavior, political opinion, and decision making. This emphasis usually meant overlooking the city itself as a factor affecting political phenomena. Only quite recently have political scientists begun to design research to determine whether political phenomena vary with the characteristics of cities or independently of city characteristics.[7]

Still another factor in redirecting the study of urban politics was the political scientist's growing insistence upon applying scientific criteria and methods to his own discipline. From the scientific perspective, broad-scale comparisons are essential to making valid generalizations

---

[6] See Robert C. Wood, "The Contributions of Political Science to Urban Form," in Hirsch, *Urban Life and Form,* pp. 115–17.

[7] The scientific importance of this kind of research is discussed in Albert J. Reiss, Jr., "The Sociological Study of Communities," *Rural Sociology* (June 1959), pp. 118–30.

(suggesting to the urban political scientist that his field needed more comparative analysis); the study of what ought to be is a matter of norms, not facts (implying that the earlier reformist literature was not scientific); and cities can be treated as units of analysis (suggesting that community variations in political phenomena might prove a fruitful area for research).

Until recently, the subject most frequently studied in the scientific literature on urban politics has been community power structure. Community power studies typically view the city as a system of influence relationships and politics as the operation of the system. The main question posed in these studies is, "Who governs?" The analyst's goal is to describe empirically the total power structure of the city, and his analysis is directed at describing powerful individuals and their characteristics, interactions, resources, and activities. Recently, however, the urban field has experienced a shift in emphasis. Increasing interest is being expressed in attempts to explain policies. Policy analysis is now being directed at hypotheses about environmental and system determinants of expenditure levels, political forms (such as city-manager governments), and specific programs. This book itself is evidence of the growing concern with policy explanation.

Why Political Scientists Study Policy

Why do political scientists study policy? One reason is that policies, reflecting as they do a political system's allocation of values, are obviously within political scientists' immediate purview. Policies also reflect people's goals for government, though not always the goals of the majority; often they reflect only the goals of community influentials, of small numbers of public officials or private citizens. Another reason for political scientists' interest in policy is that it represents an object of conflict and thus is at the heart of politics. We have already noted that for years the study of urban politics overlooked political conflict in city life (including conflict over policy) while stressing efficient provision of services and proper forms of government. In contrast, community power studies stressed policy controversies and influences on policy decisions. Recent policy studies, moreover, are rich in their coverage of conflicts and cleavages. In some recent studies differences among urbanites in terms of race, residence, income, and life style are conceptualized as indicators of conflict and examined for their relationship with policy. In other studies the policy attitudes of citizens, officials, and community influentials reveal diversity and conflict. Conflicts over the nature of governmental institutions, how much the city will spend on planning, whose street will be paved, who will bear the cost—all these conflicts are covered here.

The variable to be explained, urban policy, is defined as actions or decisions affecting the scope of governmental activity, the institutions of government, or other community-wide institutions. We do not assert that all government decisions produce change. Decisions may deliberately reinforce the status quo or leave it unaltered (e.g., "nondecisions"). Nor do we claim that policy is determined solely by those having the legitimate and recognized right to make it.[8] Policy can also be determined by persons outside the official governmental framework (as, for example, when influential "others" control government officials). Almost all the policies covered here were formally promulgated by actors within the political system. But this is not to say that recognized government officials in fact *made* the decisions or that, even if they did, they were unaffected by outside influences. Nor do we assume that all policies are determined by "elites." In referenda the masses act directly as policy makers, although their options may be limited by elites, private and public. We *do* assume that cities vary in the degree to which policies are made by elites and masses and in the degree to which elite and mass actions are influenced by environmental and political system factors. Political scientists should study all such variations.

In what ways can institutional changes be regarded as policy changes? First, since they often take place through the existing political system, institutional changes can legitimately be treated as system outputs. Also, institutions may reflect community (or dominant group) political goals, such as a desire for reformed government stressing efficiency. In addition, political institutions, like expenditures, can be viewed as rewards or deprivations. Evidently, institutions benefit some

---

[8] See Peter Rossi, "Community Decision-Making," in *Approaches to the Study of Politics*, ed. Roland Young (Evanston, Ill.: Northwestern University Press, 1958), p. 364.

people while disadvantaging others; otherwise they would not be so strenuously supported and opposed. Research suggests, for example, that unreformed political institutions (such as the mayor-council form of government) are usually supported by ethnic minorities and the working class.[9] Ethnic minorities have little or no influence based on their social position and appear to see the frankly political character of the mayor-council form as giving them more influence, or at least greater access to influence.

This book treats political institutions as policy outcomes of communities that vary in their environmental and political system characteristics and in the degree to which extracommunity forces act upon them. The term "structural policy outcomes" is hereafter used to characterize decisions that establish formal authority structures.[10]

A Way to Think About Policy Explanation

Empirical studies of urban policy have become very abundant, as the following chapters will attest. In fact, the profusion of materials has made it difficult to grasp the major themes of the literature. One study focuses on the adoption of fluoridated water supplies and isolates factors associated with adoption; another concerns consolidated city-counties and their correlates; another treats the question of segregated school systems; and still another attempts to specify the factors affecting expenditures for schools, streets, and water. The organization of this book provides a methodical way of thinking about policy explanation. A systems approach is used to order the findings of numerous studies and to help the reader develop an understanding of what recent research suggests about explanatory concepts in the study of city policies. If the reader also manages to retain the conclusions of individual studies, so much the better.

---

[9] Daniel N. Gordon, "Immigrants and Urban Government Form in American Cities, 1933–1960," *American Journal of Sociology* (September 1968), pp. 158–71, and Edwin O. Stone and George K. Floro, *Abandonments of the Manager Plan* (Lawrence: University of Kansas Publications, 1953).

[10] This use is borrowed from Robert H. Salisbury and John P. Heinz, "A Theory of Policy Analysis and Some Preliminary Applications" (Paper delivered at the 1968 meeting of the American Political Science Association, Washington, D.C.).

Until recently most attempts at generalizing about the nature of urban political phenomena preceded an operational model of the urban polity. By operational model, we mean one that accommodates the available data while suggesting ways and means of measuring phenomena accurately. A systems framework provides such a model. Directly or indirectly, many of the studies reported in this book use a systems framework. This use by contemporary researchers demonstrates that systems analysis is helpful in explaining policies. In one sense, of course, a systems perspective is basic to all scientific research. Whenever one distinguishes between the objects to be studied, the forces acting upon those objects, and the consequences of the forces, he is thinking in terms of systems. The present author does not intend to promote any particular version of systems analysis in this book. Like many others, I simply find thinking in terms of systems useful.

Systems analysis holds that cities and city governments can be scientifically described and classified in much the same way as other phenomena in the broad class "social systems." "What is known about [cities] can be systematically related to what is known about other social systems and further, what is known about other social systems may afford rich hypothetical material for further community research."[11] At the same time, one can argue that the city *is* a system in the sense that its parts (neighborhoods, social classes, businesses) are functionally interdependent and its boundaries (both the physical one separating it from the outside world and the functional one separating its government from the other community institutions) are relatively distinct.

A general systems framework is shown in Figure 1–1. It treats city government (the political system) as an interrelated set of structures and processes that encounter environmental stimuli and respond with "outputs" of goods, services, and deprivations. Stimuli are transmitted to the political system by "inputs" of two types, demands and supports. Supports are sustaining attitudes or actions that buttress the political system and add to its stability. These may develop in response to a government's policy output or may exist independently of that out-

---

[11] Roland L. Warren, *The Community in America* (Chicago: Rand McNally, 1963), p. 48. See also Irwin T. Sanders, *The Community: An Introduction to a Social System* (New York: Ronald Press, 1966).

Figure 1–1   A Political System, Its Environment and Output

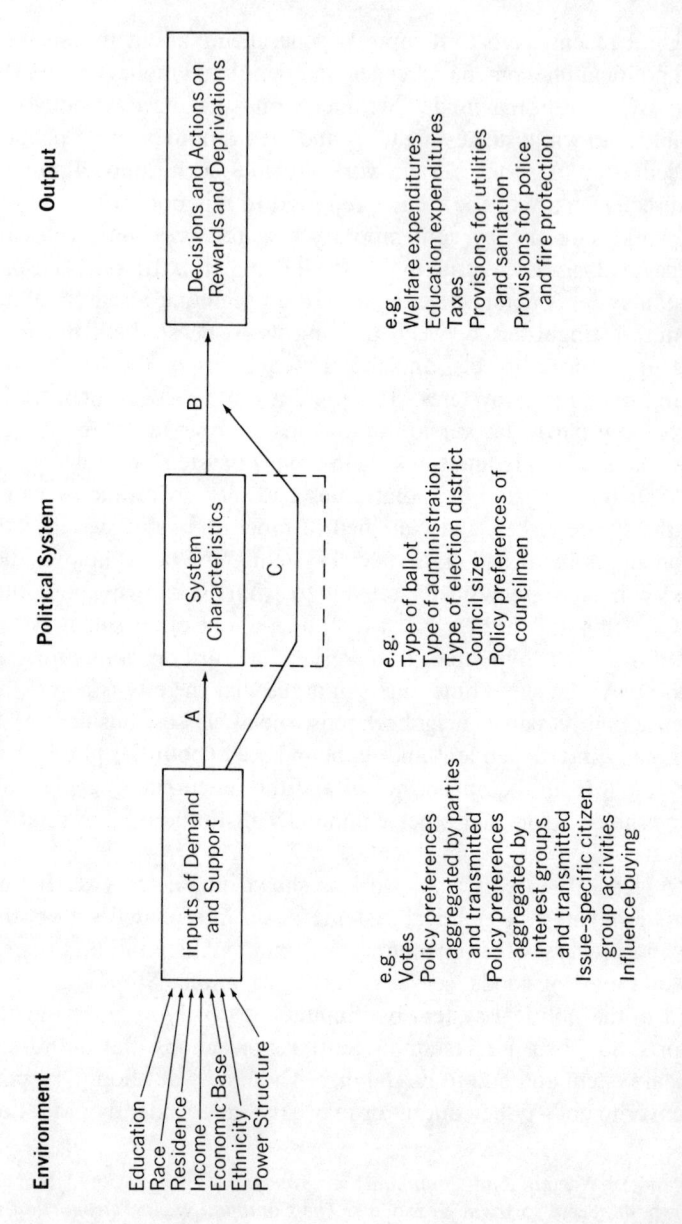

Environment	Political System	Output
Education Race Residence Income Economic Base Ethnicity Power Structure	Inputs of Demand and Support → A → System Characteristics → B →	Decisions and Actions on Rewards and Deprivations

e.g.
Votes
Policy preferences aggregated by parties and transmitted
Policy preferences aggregated by interest groups and transmitted
Issue-specific citizen group activities
Influence buying

e.g.
Type of ballot
Type of administration
Type of election district
Council size
Policy preferences of councilmen

e.g.
Welfare expenditures
Education expenditures
Taxes
Provisions for utilities and sanitation
Provisions for police and fire protection

NOTE: Line C shows a direct impact of inputs on outputs, independent of the characteristics of the political system. Lines A and B show a set of relationships in which inputs shape system characteristics, which in turn shape the policy decisions that are made.

put. Demands are forms of behavior that call for action by decision makers. Demands may be made for increased services, changes in institutions or programs, or restrictions on persons or groups.

The reader will note that line C of Figure 1–1 depicts a direct linkage between outputs and inputs, independent of the characteristics of the political system. Lines A and B, however, depict a set of relationships in which inputs shape system characteristics, which in turn affect the policy decisions that are made. Research results confirm the existence of both linkages. Many studies indicate that environmental or socioeconomic factors shape policy output directly and that political system characteristics have little independent effect, even though policies are formulated or promulgated through the system. Other studies show that system characteristics significantly affect policy outputs.

In challenge to the relationships suggested by lines A and B one sometimes hears the objection that current environmental factors could not possibly be a cause of system characteristics, such as form of government, created years before. That is quite true, but the contemporary environment could affect the *retention* of political forms—such as the mayor—established years ago. In addition, current environmental conditions could affect the way the system *actually functions* to produce outputs. The contemporary environment might affect the way existing institutions mobilize bias in favor of particular population groups. The key question is the system's policy responsiveness to the inputs of different population groups under different structural and processual arrangements.

Figure 1–2 differentiates the main classes of explanatory (i.e., "independent") variables covered in this book. The first three boxes depict the classes of variables that form the basis of the organization of *Politics and Urban Policies*. Examples of each class are listed in Table 1–1. The first box in Figure 1–2 represents extracommunity variables (forces outside the urban community) that affect policy outcomes in the community. These influences are discussed in Chapter 5. Urban sociologists, economists, and political scientists agree that the city is shaped to an important degree by extracommunity forces. The city's economy is affected by the national economy; branch businesses are influenced by the policies of their parent concerns; the city's governmental structure is influenced by state laws; local attitudes are col-

Figure 1-2 Relationships and Variables in Urban Policy Research

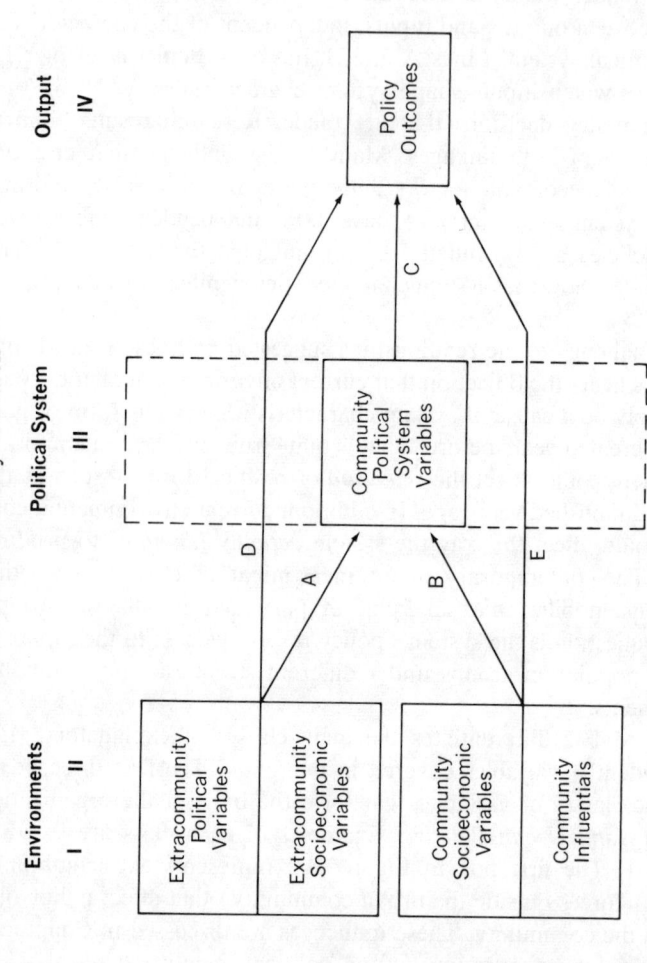

Environments	Political System	Output
I II	III	IV

Extracommunity Political Variables
Extracommunity Socioeconomic Variables

Community Socioeconomic Variables
Community Influentials

Community Political System Variables

Policy Outcomes

A
B
C
D
E

NOTE: Lines A, B, and C show environmental variables shaping system characteristics (discussed in Chapter 2), which in turn shape policy outcomes (discussed in Chapter 4). Lines D and E show environmental variables directly affecting policy (treated in Chapter 3 and 5) without sizable influence by system characteristics.

Table 1–1 Examples of Variables in Figure 1–2

I. Extracommunity Variables	II. Community Environmental Variables	III. Urban Political System Variables	IV. Urban Policy Outcome Variables
1. Federal grants-in-aid	1. Racial, ethnic composition of population	1. Form of administration	1. Level of welfare expenditures
2. State laws on governmental structure	2. Economic base	2. Type of election	2. Level of taxation
3. National political party ties	3. Educational level	3. Type of election district	3. Level of general expenditures
4. State of national economy	4. Density of population	4. Council decision-making processes	4. Urban renewal program completions
5. Absentee ownership of local corporations	5. Population growth rate	5. Degree of governmental fragmentation	5. Fluoridated water supplies
6. Regional political values and culture	6. Activities of non-governmental elites	6. Attitudes of officeholders	6. Segregated school systems

ored by the culture of the region; and local policies (on urban renewal, for example) are often importantly shaped by federal incentives. These vertical ties emphasize the dependent nature of the urban community and the fact that the city is subject to constraints by "higher and more inclusive units of decision."[12]

"Although it has been recognized that every community is a part of the larger society," notes one observer, "it has not been equally emphasized that the larger society is a part of every community. This is more than a play on words," he continues.

> A clear recognition of the way institutions of the larger society are "built into" every community, and behavior patterns of the larger society are enacted in every community, will make possible a somewhat different model of the relationship of community to larger society. It makes possible a realization that the larger society need not be "related" by the investigator to the local community, for it is already there. It is there in local cultural patterns, such as family living norms and behavior patterns which are local embodiments or enactments of parts of the culture of the larger society; and it is there in the form of social systems, such as churches, businesses, and governmental units, which are intimately related in a systematic manner to larger social systems which extend across numerous communities.[13]

One of the implications of extracommunity ties is that part of the power to make decisions affecting the community resides elsewhere, thereby impairing local autonomy.[14]

Attention to extracommunity variables requires one to distinguish between the internal relationships of urban institutions and those that penetrate the community's boundaries. In other words, we may study both the internal processes of the urban community and its functioning within the larger society. Extracommunity relationships are perhaps more clearly seen when one thinks about subsystems.[15]

---

[12] Matthew Holden, Jr., "On the Theory of Community Politics: An Essay on Reconstruction," Part III, p. 7, unpublished manuscript. Quoted by permission.

[13] Warren, *The Community in America*, p. 239.

[14] *Ibid.*, p. 65.

[15] See *ibid.*, p. 241, and Holden, "On the Theory of Community Politics." "When systems comprising groups of individuals, whether formally or informally structured, are considered in their interrelationship as units of a still larger social

It may be helpful to view cities as made up of several subsystems, such as political, economic, cultural, and social subsystems. Thinking about economic subsystems calls attention, for example, to the relationship between a national corporation as the larger system and its local subsidiaries as subsystems.

The second box in Figure 1–2 represents community environmental variables. In Chapter 3 two types of community environmental variables are discussed. One is socioeconomic variables, such as the composition of the population and community economic base. It is here that the voluminous findings showing the policy impact of ethnicity, class, religion, community size, and so on are presented. The other type of community environmental variable discussed in Chapter 3 calls attention to nongovernmental, unofficial influentials. It is here that the elitist findings on community power structure are fitted into our model, with emphasis on the impact of nonofficial actors on the policy outcomes of communities.

The third box in Figure 1–2 represents the variables of the political system, which earlier was defined as an interrelated set of structures and processes that encounter environmental stimuli and respond with policy outcomes. Chapter 4, which covers political system variables, presents evidence concerning the impact on policy of the processes, actors, and formal structures of city governments.

The fourth box represents the policy output of urban political systems. At some point, of course, all policies are the result of choice-making activities by an identifiable group of men with formally endowed prerogatives.[16] However, these activities vary in the degree to which they are shaped by environmental and political system variables. Almost all the policy outcomes described in this book came through the official institutions of government, i.e., through the political system. In some cases, however, official institutions and behaviors had little or no independent effect on the decisions made.

---

system, they are often designated as subsystems. This indicates that they themselves are social systems, but at the same time they are parts of a larger social system." Warren, *The Community in America*, p. 138.

[16] Richard I. Hofferbert, "Elite Influence in Policy Formation: A Model for Comparative Inquiry" (Paper delivered at the 1968 meeting of the American Political Science Association, Washington, D.C.).

The approach taken in this book, to sum up, calls attention to three main classes of phenomena: environmental (both extracommunity and community) variables, political system variables, and policy output variables.

chapter 2
The Environmental Base of Urban Governmental Forms

Cities vary according to governmental administration (whether manager, mayor, or commission), electoral system (partisan or nonpartisan), election district (at-large, ward, or a combination of the two), and the presence or absence of "integrative governments" (such as consolidated city-counties or metropolitan special districts). Political scientists try to account for these differences by determining the conditions associated with each form. What evidence is available about the conduciveness of different environments to the various forms? Does it make sense empirically to say that each form is found most frequently in environments conducive to it?[1] If so, which environments are conducive to which forms?

In studying the environmental base of urban governmental forms one customarily distinguishes between "reformed" and "unreformed" institutions. The classic reformed institutions include a city-manager form of government, nonpartisan elections, and at-large constituencies. Some writers suggest that large constituencies, small councils, and

[1] See John H. Kessel, "Governmental Structure and Political Environment: A Statistical Note about American Cities," *American Political Science Review* (September 1962), pp. 615–20.

broad civil service coverage of employees also typify reformed government. Other analysts assert that integrative governments belong in the reformed category—that they represent the latest good government device in the long line of reformist notions.[2] The main components of *unreformed* governments are a mayor, partisan elections, and ward constituencies. Some commentators also note that unreformed governments characteristically have small constituencies, large councils, and comparatively little civil service coverage.[3]

Reformed institutions were originally designed to remove politics from local government in order to stress technical and managerial standards in the provision of services. For this reason reformed governments are often called "professionalized." Unreformed governments, on the other hand, are said to encourage or to allow group representation, political bargaining, and interest arbitration. For this reason they are called "politicized." Theory suggests that unreformed institutions reflect a competing variety of group goals,[4] while reformed institutions reflect middle class goals, such as the priority of government's service-providing function. Where there is more diversity in a city's population —whether ethnic, racial, or social diversity—there tends to be more disagreement about the goals that government ought to pursue. Indeed, there tends to be conflict over goals, which in turn generates pressures for "politicized," "group arbitrating" forms of government that are more responsive to traditional groups' desires for access and influence.

To sum up, cities vary in their formal political institutions and in the environments of those institutions. There is, in addition, a body of theory linking political institutions with their environments. This theory stresses the political impact of population diversity.

---

[2] See Raymond E. Wolfinger and John Osgood Field, "Political Ethos and the Structure of City Government," *American Political Science Review* (June 1966), pp. 306–26, and Norton Long, "Recent Theories and Problems of Local Government," *Public Policy*, eds. Carl J. Friedrich and Seymour E. Harris (Cambridge: Harvard Graduate School of Public Administration, 1958), 285–95.

[3] See Wolfinger and Field, "Political Ethos and City Government," on the last item.

[4] Kessel, "Governmental Structure and Political Environment," and Robert R. Alford and Harry M. Scoble, "Political and Socioeconomic Characteristics of American Cities," in *Municipal Yearbook* (Chicago: International City Managers' Association, 1965), pp. 82–97.

Ethnicity

One characteristic of the community environment that is closely related to governmental form is the ethnic composition of the population. When cities are compared, it is found that increases in the proportion of foreign-born or foreign stock[5] persons coincide with increases in the incidence of unreformed political institutions. In other words, there is a positive correlation between ethnicity and unreformed institutions, especially mayoral government. One study shows an ethnicity–mayoral form correlation over many years.[6] Table 2–1 shows that foreign-born population was a correlate of the mayoral form in 1933 and was still a correlate of that form in 1960. Further analysis (See Table 2–2) shows that this relationship persists under controls for region, city economic base, population size, and population change. Also, this analysis indicates that there was a resurgence of the immigrant influence on governmental forms between 1950 and 1960. These findings are especially important in that the analysis on which they are based spanned a considerable amount of time, covered many cities, and controlled for other possible influences on governmental form. All 1930 cities over 30,000, 94 percent of 1960 cities over 25,000, and 75 percent of 1960 cities over 50,000 are included in the study. According to the study's author, the findings are probably applicable to all cities with a 1960 population greater than 25,000.[7]

Comparative studies at one point in time also support generalizations about an ethnicity–unreformed institutions link. Robert R. Alford and Harry M. Scoble find foreign parentage to be associated with the mayoral form of government, independent of nonwhite composition and population mobility. They conclude that "ethnic groups of European origin" are important sources of social heterogeneity related to

---

[5] "Foreign stock" means native-born persons of foreign or mixed native and foreign parentage. One or both parents have to be foreign born for an individual to be in this category.

[6] Daniel N. Gordon, "Immigrants and Urban Governmental Form in American Cities, 1933–1960," *American Journal of Sociology* (September 1968), pp. 158–71.

[7] *Ibid.*, p. 164.

Table 2–1 Form of Government in 1933, 1940, 1950, and 1960
by the Percentage of Foreign-Born Persons
in 1930, 1940, 1950, and 1960, Respectively
(N = 268)

Form of Government	Percentage of Foreign Born			
	Low (0-5%)	Medium (6-14%)	High (15-37%)	Total
1933 ($V = .259$):				
Mayor-council (wards)[a]	22	33	58	42
Mayor-council (at-large)	8	5	7	7
Commission[b]	29	27	22	25
Council-manager (wards)	7	6	2	4
Council-manager (at-large)	34	29	10	22
Total	100 (N = 76)	100 (N = 66)	99[c] (N = 125)	100 (N = 267)[d]
1940 ($V = .271$):				
Mayor-council (wards)	25	37	61	41
Mayor-council (at-large)	7	4	12	8
Commission	27	26	18	24
Council-manager (wards)	11	5	1	6
Council-manager (at-large)	30	28	8	22
Total	100 (N = 83)	100 (N = 93)	100 (N = 92)	101[c] (N = 268)
1950 ($V = .188$):				
Mayor-council (wards)	26	43	48	38
Mayor-council (at-large)	9	4	13	8
Commission	20	21	20	20
Council-manager (wards)	12	6	4	8
Council-manager (at-large)	34	26	15	26
Total	101[c] (N = 101)	100 (N = 94)	100 (N = 71)	100 (N = 266)[e]

Table 2–1 (*continued*)

Form of Government	Percentage of Foreign Born			
	Low (0-5%)	Medium (6-14%)	High (15-37%)	Total
1960 ($V = .288$):				
Mayor-council (wards)	17	49	41	34
Mayor-council (at-large)	9	6	24	9
Commission	16	11	21	14
Council-manager (wards)	16	7	0	10
Council-manager (at-large)	41	27	14	32
Total	99[c]	100	100	99[c]
	(N = 117)	(N = 118)	(N = 29)	(N = 264)[f]

[a] Wards means that some or all of the city councilmen are elected from wards. Data sources for the forms of government and council elections were obtained from the *Municipal Yearbook* for the years 1934 (Table I), 1941 (Table II), 1951 (Table III), and 1961 (Table IV). All these volumes were published in Chicago by the International City Managers' Association in 1934, 1941, 1951, and 1961, respectively. Since the data reported in these books are for January in the year they were published, the governmental data really reflect the governmental forms existing in the previous year.

[b] Commission government, by definition, has no wards.

[c] Rounding error.

[d] One city did not report its form of council elections.

[e] Two cities did not report their form of council elections.

[f] Four cities did not report their form of council elections.

SOURCE: Daniel N. Gordon, "Immigrants and Urban Governmental Form in American Cities, 1933–1960," *American Journal of Sociology* (September 1968), p. 166. Reprinted by permission of The University of Chicago Press.

form of government.[8] Robert L. Lineberry and Edmund P. Fowler find that cities administered by mayors have a higher ethnic population than those administered by city managers or commissions. They further show that cities holding partisan elections have a higher concentration of ethnic minorities than do those characterized by nonpartisan

[8] Alford and Scoble, "Characteristics of American Cities," pp. 93–96. All 1960 cities over 25,000 are included in their analysis. See also Kessel, "Governmental Structure and Political Environment."

Table 2-2 Cramer's V for the Relationship
Between the Percentage of Foreign-Born Persons
and Governmental Form with and without Control Variables,
for the Years 1933, 1940, 1950, and 1960

Control Variable	Year			
	1933	1940	1950	1960
None	.259	.271	.188	.288
Region:				
East[a]	.271	.177	.146	.245
Midwest[b]	.165	.252	.289	.438
West[c]	.340	.485	.376	.339
South[d]	.253	.157	.221	.199
Percentage employed in manufacturing:				
Low (16-38)[e]	.215	.272	.218	.238
Medium (39-48)	.306	.202	.209	.278
High (49-80)	.270	.403	.212	.491
Population size:				
Small (25,000-52,000)[f]	.304	.275	.320	.340
Medium (53,000-94,000)	.219	.241	.220	.423
Large (95,000 or more)	.306	.337	.226	.278
Proportion population change:[g]				
Decrease–small increase (0.032-1.495)	.266	.214	.162	.306
Medium increase (1.496-2.156)	.305	.453	.367	.484
Large increase (2.157-71.00)	.315	.547	.375	.336[h]

NOTE: Cramer's V indicates the degree to which variables are related to one another.

[a] The eastern states are Maine, New Hampshire, Massachusetts, Connecticut, Rhode Island, New York, New Jersey, Maryland, and Delaware. No Vermont cities were in the sample because of their small size. Pennsylvania cities were eliminated from the sample.

[b] The midwestern states are Ohio, Illinois, Wisconsin, Minnesota, Iowa, South Dakota, and Nebraska. No North Dakota cities were in the sample because of their small size. Indiana cities were eliminated from the sample.

[c] The western states are Montana, Colorado, Utah, Arizona, California, Oregon, and Washington. No Idaho, Wyoming, New Mexico, Nevada, Alaska, or Hawaii cities were included in the sample because their cities were too small in 1933.

[d] The southern states are Texas, Oklahoma, Kansas, Missouri, Arkansas, Louisiana, Mississippi, Florida, Georgia, North Carolina, South Carolina, Virginia, West Virginia, Kentucky, and Tennessee. Alabama cities were eliminated from the sample.

[e] The percentage employed in manufacturing was obtained by dividing the total employed labor force into the number of workers in manufacturing and mechanical industries (1930) and by dividing the total employed labor force into the total number

Table 2–2 (*continued*)

---

of craftsmen, foremen and kindred workers, and operatives and kindred workers (1940, 1950, and 1960). Although the census categories of occupations changed between 1930 and 1940, 1950, and 1960, the three latter years appear to be close enough to the 1930 definition to make a meaningful comparison. The data sources for occupation were as follows: 1930: U.S. Bureau of the Census, *Population,* Vol. IV: *Occupations by States* (Washington: U.S. Government Printing Office, 1932), Tables 4 and 5; 1940: U.S. Bureau of the Census, *Population,* Vol. II: *Characteristics of the Population* (Washington: U.S. Government Printing Office, 1943), Table 33 (cities less than 100,000 population), and Vol. III: *The Labor Force,* Table 11 (cities with populations of 100,000 or more); 1950: U.S. Bureau of the Census, *Census of Population: 1950,* Vol. II: *Characteristics of the Population* (Washington: U.S. Government Printing Office, 1952), Table 35; 1960: U.S. Bureau of the Census, *Census of Population: 1960,* Vol. I:*Characteristics of the Population* (Washington: U.S. Government Printing Office, 1963), Table 74.

The low-, medium-, and high-percentage categories of the labor force employed in manufacturing were derived in the same manner as the population-size categories.

[f] The data sources for population size were as follows: 1930: U.S. Bureau of the Census, *Population,* Vol. III: *Reports by States* (Washington: U.S. Government Printing Office, 1932), Table 15; 1940: U.S. Bureau of the Census, *Population,* Vol. II (cited in n. e above), Tables 31 and 34; 1950: U.S. Bureau of the Census, *Census of Population: 1950,* Vol. II (cited in n. e above), Table 35; 1960: U.S. Bureau of the Census, *Census of Population: 1960,* Vol. I (cited in n. e above), Table 34. These sources were also used to obtain the percentages of foreign-born persons.

[g] The proportion of population change from 1900 to 1930 was used as the control variable for 1933. For 1940, 1950, and 1960 the proportion population change for 1930–60 was used. The category boundaries were obtained in the same manner as those for population size. The data source for 1900 population (from which change 1900–1930 was computed) was the U.S. Census Office, *Population,* Part I (Washington: U.S. Census Office, 1901), Table 8. A few cities were not incorporated in 1900. Population size for them was first obtained for 1910 from the U.S. Bureau of the Census, *Population, 1910* (Washington: U.S. Government Printing Office, 1913), Tables II and III.

[h] Since Cramer's *V* does not give the direction of association, the reader should be informed that this association was the reverse of all the others.

SOURCE: Daniel N. Gordon, "Immigrants and Urban Governmental Form in American Cities, 1933–1960," *American Journal of Sociology* (September 1968), p. 168. Reprinted by permission of The University of Chicago Press.

elections and that cities divided into ward constituencies are comparatively more ethnic in population than those with at-large constituencies.[9] In addition, analysis of 300 suburban communities lying within

---

[9] Robert L. Lineberry and Edmund P. Fowler, "Reformism and Public Policies in American Cities," *American Political Science Review* (September 1967), p. 705. This analysis is based on a random sample of 200 of the 309 cities with 50,000 or more population in 1960.

the 25 largest urbanized areas reveals similar associations: there is a greater percentage of foreign-born persons in mayor-run than in manager-run cities.[10]

On the other hand, race does not discriminate between reformed and unreformed cities in a way consistent with theory stressing the political impact of population diversity. There are proportionately more nonwhites in manager-run than in mayor-run cities, still more in commission-run cities, and more in cities with at-large than ward elections. However, the expected relationship is found with respect to election types: partisan cities have proportionately more nonwhites than nonpartisan cities.[11] In the suburbs there is a somewhat higher percentage of nonwhites in mayor-run than in manager-run communities and an even higher percentage in commission-run communities.[12]

At least one interesting challenge has been posed to the linking of ethnic population and unreformed institutions. Wolfinger and Field find that mayor-administered cities have higher proportions of foreign stock than do manager-run cities; but when this relationship is examined by region the association is substantially reduced. In the Northeast the proportions of ethnic populations in mayor- and manager-run cities are virtually the same. In the Midwest and West mayor-run cities have slightly higher ethnic concentrations. And when partisan elections (another important component of reformed government) are examined on a regional basis, their positive correlation with ethnicity is sharply reversed in the Northeast and is attenuated in the Midwest and West. When the type of constituency is considered, we find that both ward and at-large cities in the Northeast have comparable ethnic populations, while in the West at-large cities have a *higher* percentage of ethnic strains than ward cities. Given these attenuated and reversed associations whenever a regional breakdown is provided, Raymond E. Wolfinger and John Osgood Field suggest that one can more accurately predict a city's political forms by knowing its location than by knowing

---

[10] Commission-run cities have a still larger percentage. Leo F. Schnore and Robert R. Alford, "Forms of Government and Socioeconomic Characteristics of Suburbs," *Administrative Science Quarterly* (June 1963), p. 12.

[11] Lineberry and Fowler, "Reformism and Public Policies," pp. 705–706.

[12] Schnore and Alford, "Forms of Government," p. 12.

its population composition.[13] They assert that research findings about the influence of ethnicity (which appear in their national data as well as in others') are spurious and represent merely an artifact of region.[14] An important question, however, is the usefulness of the variable "region" in explaining the incidence of particular governmental forms as compared with that of more narrowly specific variables like ethnic and class composition. This subject will be discussed at greater length later in this chapter.

In any case, having demonstrated an association between ethnicity and unreformed institutions, the next task is to explain it. Why might such an association exist? What is there about communities having a greater concentration of ethnic groups that might be conducive to the retention of "politicized" institutions? One explanation is offered by John H. Kessel. He argues that ethnic groups are especially dependent on political activities for their advancement because they have been excluded from alternative and more conventional means of advancement, i.e., from wealth and social standing.[15] When a group lacks wealth and social standing, he asserts, its members come to value access to government, public officeholding, and patronage. This means that the group will prefer "frankly political" governmental forms to those intended to remove political bargaining from the local scene. In short, a higher proportion of ethnic minorities indexes a felt need for political opportunities of advancement, which unreformed institutions better provide. Whether or not ethnic groups actually perceive unreformed governments to be in their interest is a question as yet unanswered by sample survey data.

A similar explanation of the ethnicity–unreformed institutions link simply stresses human and goal diversity. When there is more diversity in a city's population, there tends to be more conflict over the goals that government ought to pursue and thus over policy. Greater conflict over city policy results in pressures to retain unreservedly political institutions offering greater access to population groups.

[13] Wolfinger and Field, "Political Ethos and City Government."

[14] Other studies also show a relationship of region to form of government. Different regional locations are associated with a differential use of reformed institutions. Alford and Scoble, "Characteristics of American Cities," pp. 89–90, and Schnore and Alford, "Forms of Government," p. 9.

[15] Kessel, "Governmental Structure and Political Environment."

Class

Another kind of heterogeneity that is related to political structure is class standing. Of course, theory stressing the explanatory importance of human differences and research suggesting that higher ethnic concentrations produce pressures for governmental forms amenable to group access lead one to assume that class diversity and working class standing might produce the same pressures. A high proportion of working class persons should be associated with politicized forms because such persons are more likely to have political demands inconsistent with professionalized forms;[16] that is, they are less likely to share the goals of efficiency and economy and more likely to countenance political bargaining and to feel the need for political means of advancement.

However, the findings on the relationship of class to political forms are not consistently patterned. Using different measures of "class" (e.g., type of occupation, level of education, amount of annual income, and type of dwelling) and studying different populations, various researchers have reported conflicting findings.

An intricate quantitative analysis of the correlates of reform government, measured by an index scoring cities according to the number of classic reform characteristics present, reveals "highly educated population" to be the strongest correlate. Even when such factors as population size, economic diversification, Catholic population percentage, and civic organization activity are considered, highly educated population still emerges as the main statistical explanation.[17]

A study of charter reform outcomes in twenty-five Pennsylvania cities discloses a positive correlation between class measures and adoption of new charters. The Pennsylvania study, however, categorizes adoptions of mayoral and manager forms together under "charter reform" because both represent changes from the commission form,

[16] Alford and Scoble, "Characteristics of American Cities," p. 83.
[17] Terry N. Clark, "Community Structure, Decision-Making, Budget Expenditures, and Urban Renewal in 51 American Communities," *American Sociological Review* (August 1968), p. 584.

which until 1957 had been required by state law. Thus it is not fully comparable with the other studies cited here.[18]

In the nation's suburbs the popular image of the manager-administered community appears to be true; suburbs are the "natural habitat of the upper middle class,"[19] concludes one study. Another study finds that in cities over 25,000 a city-manager form of government consistently correlates with higher education levels.[20] Moreover, at least two case studies of community conflict over governmental forms report working class support of unreformed institutions.[21]

On the other hand, one analysis of a random sample of cities with a 1960 population over 50,000 concludes that reformed cities are not the natural habitat of the middle class. The data show very little difference in the class composition of reformed and unreformed cities.[22] The same negative findings appear in a study of all cities over 50,000. When examined within regions, measures of class (occupation, income, and education) do not substantially discriminate between reformed and unreformed cities, although there is directional support of the theory in most two-variable relationships. (The ability of the class measures to discriminate between reformed and unreformed cities nationwide is not reported.[23]) In addition, an even more extensive comparative study shows that although cities with higher proportions of white-collar workers are far more likely to have managers than cities with low proportions, when population mobility is considered, the latter

[18] James W. Clarke, "Environment, Process and Policy: A Reconsideration," *American Political Science Review* (December 1969), Table 3.

[19] Schnore and Alford, "Forms of Government," p. 15. See also Edgar L. Sherbenou, "Class, Participation, and the Council-Manager Plan," *Public Administration Review* (Summer 1961), pp. 131–35.

[20] Alford and Scoble, "Characteristics of American Cities," p. 88.

[21] Edwin O. Stone and George K. Floro, *Abandonments of the Manager Plan* (Lawrence: University of Kansas Publications, 1953), and Robert E. Agger, Daniel Goldrich, and Bert E. Swanson, *The Rulers and the Ruled* (New York: Wiley, 1964), p. 673.

[22] Lineberry and Fowler, "Reformism and Public Policies."

[23] When examining the class-form relationship, the Wolfinger-Field study controls not only for region but also for population size when type of administration (in cities of 50,000-500,000) and type of constituency (in cities of 50,000-1,000,000) are analyzed.

"appears to explain the association of economic and class composition with form."[24] (See Table 2–4.)

Economic Base

Related to the class composition of a city is its economic base. Economic base refers to the nature of the local economy, whether the emphasis is on manufacturing, retail trade, personal services, or diversification.[25] The council-manager form of government appears less frequently in industrial and manufacturing cities than in retail and diversified ones.[26] Among medium-size cities the manager plan is most popular in those emphasizing, respectively, personal services, professional services, retail trade, finance, public administration, wholesale trade, diversified industries, transportation, and manufacturing (see Figure 2–1). Stressing the nature of the labor force, Kessel interprets these findings in a way that accords with theory linking higher socioeconomic standing and reformed institutions. Industrial laborers, he suggests, may suffer the same kind of exclusion from social and economic means of advancement as do ethnic groups, and thus they may be similarly dependent on political channels.[27] Also, he points out, cities with managers have an economic base that suggests a concentration of middle class businessmen whose principal market is likely to be local and whose businesses are likely to be locally owned.

Phillips Cutright discovers a similar relationship while studying the environmental correlates of nonpartisan electoral systems. He hypothesizes that where class "cleavages" exist in a community partisan elections will more likely be retained. Cutright reasons that durable social cleavages provide a social base conducive to the maintenance of competing party organizations. "Two-party organization is difficult to

---

[24] Alford and Scoble, "Characteristics of American Cities," p. 95.
[25] See Howard Nelson, "A Service Classification of American Cities," *Economic Geography* (July 1955), pp. 180–210, and issues of the *Municipal Yearbook* (Chicago: International City Managers' Association).
[26] Alford and Scoble "Characteristics of American Cities," footnote 4.
[27] Kessel, "Governmental Structure and Political Environment," pp. 618–19.

Figure 2-1 Governmental Form and Economic Base: Incidence of Three Systems in Different Types of Cities

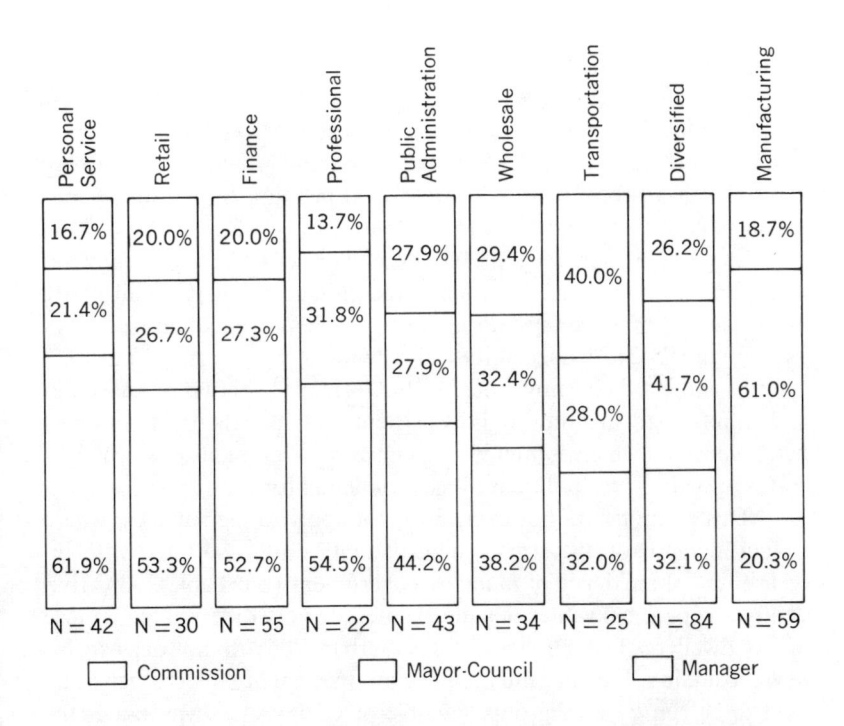

	Personal Service	Retail	Finance	Professional	Public Administration	Wholesale	Transportation	Diversified	Manufacturing
Commission	16.7%	20.0%	20.0%	13.7%	27.9%	29.4%	40.0%	26.2%	18.7%
Mayor-Council	21.4%	26.7%	27.3%	31.8%	27.9%	32.4%	28.0%	41.7%	61.0%
Manager	61.9%	53.3%	52.7%	54.5%	44.2%	38.2%	32.0%	32.1%	20.3%
	N = 42	N = 30	N = 55	N = 22	N = 43	N = 34	N = 25	N = 84	N = 59

SOURCE: John H. Kessel, "Governmental Structure and Political Environment," *American Political Science Review* (September 1962), p. 618. Reprinted by permission of the American Political Science Association.

sustain in homogeneous communities."[28] His data support the hypothesis: partisan elections are found predominantly in cities with an industrial base, while other cities tend to prefer nonpartisan elections.

A study of twenty-one suburban cities in Cook County (Chicago), Illinois, detects a similar relationship between manufacturing

[28] Phillips Cutright, "Nonpartisan Electoral Systems in American Cities." *Comparative Studies in Society and History* (January 1963), p. 218.

cities and "nonmanager" government; but the association is greatly weakened when income is held constant.[29]

Population Variables

Demographic variables are another type of environmental influence related to political structure. Population size and growth differ between cities that have reformed and unreformed institutions; so does population mobility—movement into and out of the city.

Large cities generally prefer the mayor-council form of government. Interestingly, this form also predominates in very small cities, while the city-manager system is most prevalent in medium-size cities (see Figure 2–2).[30] Large cities also tend to have partisan electoral systems and ward constituencies.[31] This correlation between large cities and unreformed institutions is consistent with the theory that social heterogeneity (which is highly correlated with population size) generates pressures for "politicized" governmental forms.

This relationship, however, does not apply to the suburbs, where in fact increases in the size of suburban cities are associated with increases in the incidence of *manager* government (see Table 2–3). Evidently, the political values of suburbanites are very different from those of city dwellers. The authors of the suburban study do not discuss this deviant finding, but one might speculate that small suburbs generally tend to be run by elite groups capable of getting their way under the existing (or perhaps any) institutional structure. In larger suburbs, on the other hand, dominant groups may see a change to reformed institutions as instrumental to the attainment of their goals.

In short, generalizations about population size and governmental form do not simply link increasing size with an increasing incidence of unreformed institutions. The evidence does not support such a gen-

---

[29] Charles S. Liebman, "Functional Differentiation and Political Characteristics of Suburbs," *American Journal of Sociology* (May 1961), pp. 485–90.

[30] Kessel, "Governmental Structure and Political Environment," p. 615; Alford and Scoble, "Characteristics of American Cities," p. 87; and Lineberry and Fowler, "Reformism and Public Policies," p. 705.

[31] Lineberry and Fowler, "Reformism and Public Policies," Table 2.

Figure 2-2 Governmental Form and Community Size

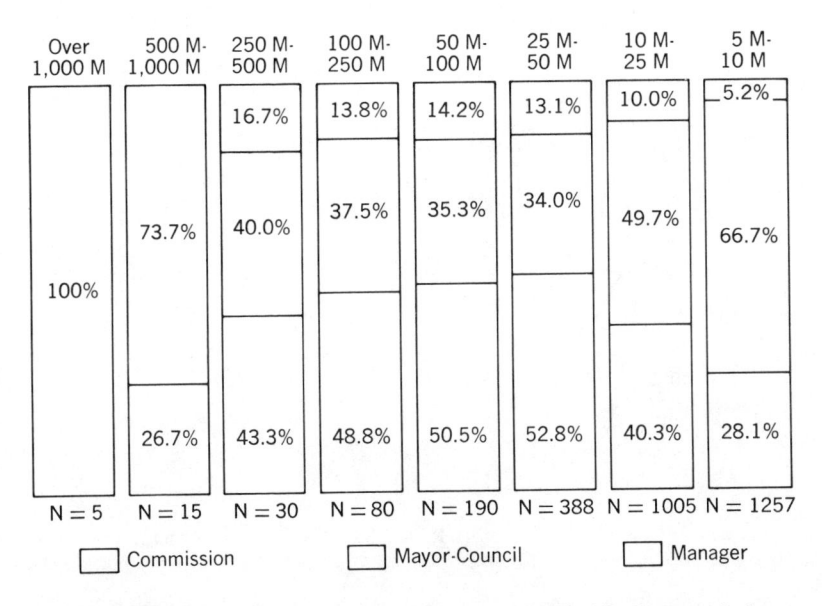

	Over 1,000 M	500 M-1,000 M	250 M-500 M	100 M-250 M	50 M-100 M	25 M-50 M	10 M-25 M	5 M-10 M
Commission (top)			16.7%	13.8%	14.2%	13.1%	10.0%	5.2%
Mayor-Council (middle)	100%	73.7%	40.0%	37.5%	35.3%	34.0%	49.7%	66.7%
Manager (bottom)		26.7%	43.3%	48.8%	50.5%	52.8%	40.3%	28.1%
N	N = 5	N = 15	N = 30	N = 80	N = 190	N = 388	N = 1005	N = 1257

☐ Commission   ☐ Mayor-Council   ☐ Manager

SOURCE: John H. Kessel, "Governmental Structure and Political Environment," *American Political Science Review* (September 1962), p. 616. Reprinted by permission of the American Political Science Association.

eralization: mayors predominate in both the largest and smallest cities, and the suburbs are a deviant case. The prevalence of the mayoral form may be explained in two ways. In larger cities the linking of human diversity, competing interests, and politicized institutions is probably the explanation. In smaller cities community values may tend to conflict with professional, city manager values, thus exerting pressures against the adoption of manager government. The popularity of the mayoral form in smaller cities, in other words, may be due to the reluctance of the local citizens to accept outside values—professionalized or not—as guides to policy making.[32]

Another population variable that differentiates reformed and unreformed cities is population growth. Fast-growing cities are likely to

---

[32] Kessel, "Governmental Structure and Political Environment," p. 616.

Table 2–3   Forms of Suburban Government by Size and Regional Location

Size and Location	% Commission	% Mayor-Council	% Council-Manager	Number
Size of suburb, 1960				
100,000 or more	12.5	37.5	50.0	16
50,000-100,000	13.8	41.4	44.8	58
25,000-50,000	13.6	39.8	46.6	103
10,000-25,000	13.8	61.0	25.2	123
Regional location				
Northeast	21.2	63.6	15.2	132
Northcentral	11.0	50.5	38.5	91
South	16.7	33.3	50.0	18
West	0.0	16.9	83.1	59
All suburbs	13.7	48.7	37.6	300

SOURCE: Leo F. Schnore and Robert R. Alford, "Forms of Government and Socioeconomic Characteristics of Suburbs," *Administrative Science Quarterly* (June 1963), p. 9. Reprinted by permission of *Administrative Science Quarterly* and the authors.

possess a manager form of government.[33] Cities with relatively low growth rates tend to have mayors,[34] and cities losing population tend to have mayor and commission forms in about equal proportions.[35] The rate of population increase also correlates positively with two other items on the reform agenda: nonpartisan elections and at-large constituencies.[36] Moreover, a similar pattern is detectable in the suburbs; that is, a faster rate of growth is associated with the council-manager form, and population loss is associated with the commission form.[37]

Related to population growth or loss is population mobility (i.e., the rate of movement in or out of a locality). Alford and Scoble the-

---

[33] Alford and Scoble, "Characteristics of American Cities," p. 86, and Kessel, "Governmental Structure and Political Environment," Figure 2.

[34] Kessel, "Governmental Structure and Political Environment," p. 616.

[35] *Ibid.*

[36] Lineberry and Fowler, "Reformism and Public Policies," Table 2.

[37] Schnore and Alford, "Forms of Government," Table 4.

orize that a highly mobile population is unlikely to form stable political groupings that compete; it is more likely to generate demands for an efficient, businesslike, service-providing government—as opposed to one responsive to traditional groups' desires for representation and access. Low mobility, conversely, implies a "population settled into stable social and political groups."[38] And the evidence in their data (covering all cities over 25,000) supports their hypothesis (see Tables 2–4 and 2–5). The manager form is most characteristic of cities with a highly mobile population. And the association persists under relevant controls: population mobility is related to form of government independently of region, class (occupation), religious diversity, ethnicity, and even population change. In addition, mobility is *more closely* related to governmental form than is occupation, population change, and ethnicity. Finally,

> mobility appears to explain the association of economic and class composition with form. It is apparently through mobility that a political base is changed, because mobile blue-collar cities are as likely to have managers as mobile white-collar cities. Similarly mobility seems to explain how population growth and decline affect form of government. It is not just growth, but primarily that fact of a sizeable mobility on the part of a city's population which destroys the potential political opposition to a professional city manager.[39] (See Tables 2–4 and 2–5.)

Thus, population mobility appears to be a key environmental variable in explaining city political system characteristics.

Religion

Another social variable importantly related to the form of city government is religion. Religious differences, like other types of diversity, appear to be associated with pressures for less professionalized and more politicized forms. Data on all cities over 25,000 population indicate that religious diversity (crudely measured by the percentage of

---

[38] Alford and Scoble, "Characteristics of American Cities," pp. 83 and 85.
[39] *Ibid.*, pp. 89, 91, and 95–96.

Table 2-4 Form of Government by Mobility and Population Change

Mobility	Population Decline High (7-29%)	Population Decline Medium (4-6%)	Population Decline Low (0-3%)	Population Growth Low (0-15%)	Population Growth Medium (16-44%)	Population Growth High (45% +)	Total
Low (2-11%)							
Manager	19%	25%	26%	25%	19%	28%	23%
Commission	40	31	16	16	11	5	22
Mayor-council	41	44	58	59	71	67	55
N =	(42)	(32)	(19)	(51)	(27)	(21)	(192)
Total	22%	17	11	27	14	11	100%
Medium (12-20%)							
Manager	—%	—%	27%	40%	47%	63%	47%
Commission	—	—	13	20	12	9	14
Mayor-council	—	—	60	40	41	28	39
N =	(8)	(8)	(15)	(83)	(93)	(43)	(250)
Total	3%	4	6	33	37	17	100%
High (21-58%)							
Manager	—%	—%	—%	72%	61%	81%	73%
Commission	—	—	—	6	15	7	9
Mayor-council	—	—	—	22	24	12	18
N =	(0)	(0)	(3)	(18)	(61)	(114)	(196)
Total	—%	—	2	9	31	58	100%

Average percentage-point difference for population change: manager, +18; mayor-council, +23. Average percentage-point difference for mobility: manager, +47; mayor-council, +46.

SOURCE: Robert R. Alford and Harry M. Scoble, "Political and Socioeconomic Characteristics of American Cities," in *Municipal Yearbook* (Chicago: International City Managers' Association, 1965), p. 92. Reprinted by permission of the publishers.

children attending private schools) is strongly associated with mayor-council government. Two-thirds of the cities with a low percentage of private school attendance have managers, while three-fifths of the cities characterized by high enrollment in private schools have mayors. Interestingly, when religious diversity and population mobility are con-

Table 2–5 Form of Government by Proportion
in White Collar Occupations and Mobility

Proportion in White Collar Occupations[a]	Low (2-11%)	Mobility Medium (12-20%)	High (21-58%)	Total
Low (15-35%)				
Manager	17%	37%	79%	32%
Commission	25	16	14	20
Mayor-council	58	47	7	48
N =	(127)	(77)	(28)	(232)
Total	55%	33	12	100%
Medium (36-42%)				
Manager	32%	46%	69%	51%
Commission	18	12	9	12
Mayor-council	50	42	22	37
N =	(38)	(96)	(67)	(201)
Total	19%	48	33	100%
High (43-85%)				
Manager	36%	57%	73%	62%
Commission	16	16	9	13
Mayor-council	48	27	18	25
N =	(25)	(74)	(94)	(193)
Total	13%	38	49	100%

[a] White collar refers to persons employed in professional, technical, managerial, clerical, and sales occupations.

Average percentage-point difference for mobility: council-manager form, +45; mayor-council +36. Average percentage-point difference for occupational composition: manager, +11; mayor-council, +6.

SOURCE: Robert R. Alford and Harry M. Scoble, "Political and Socioeconomic Characteristics of American Cities," in *Municipal Yearbook* (Chicago: International City Managers' Association, 1965), p. 91. Reprinted by permission of the publisher.

sidered together, they are additive in their effect on the form of government.

Taking both factors into account provides a high level of predictability of the form of government of a city. Of cities with the lowest mobility and the highest proportion of children in private schools, 18 percent have a manager form, 16 a commission form, 66 percent a mayor-council form, as contrasted with 78, 9, and 13 percent, respectively, in cities with highest mobility and the lowest proportion of children in private school.[40]

Religious diversity also correlates positively with partisan elections.[41] But an important factor conditioning this relationship is the nature of the local economy. When the proportion of the city's labor force employed in manufacturing is high, the difference between high- and low-percentage Catholic cities in retaining partisan elections is small. But, as Table 2–6 indicates, a significant religious difference in retaining partisan elections does show up in cities where manufacturing levels are low. One possible explanation for this phenomenon is that where class cleavages are absent religious cleavages may play an important role in maintaining partisan elections. A social base characterized by substantial diversity in religious ties thus appears to be conducive to competing party organizations. Religious cleavages, in other words, provide a favorable social base for partisan politics.[42]

Data on cities over 50,000 support these findings. Private school attendance discriminates between cities having partisan and nonpartisan elections and ward and at-large election districts. These findings too are consistent with theory linking social diversity and unreformed political institutions.

Region

The relationship of region to form of government has produced controversy and conflicting evidence. As earlier noted, Raymond E. Wolfinger and John Osgood Field's data show "striking regional variations" in the prevalence of different administrative forms. "The mayor form is the predominant one in the Northeast, is somewhat favored in the

[40] *Ibid.,* pp. 92–93.
[41] Cutright, "Nonpartisan Electoral Systems," pp. 212–26.
[42] *Ibid.,* pp. 306 and 309–310.

Table 2–6 Manufacturing Levels, Religious Composition, and Urban Electoral Systems: Competitive States Only

Percentage Holding Partisan Elections

Manufacturing Levels	High Catholic Only	Low Catholic Only	Row Differences
High	56% (N = 93)	48% (N = 60)	X^2 (1 df) = 0.8, $p < .50$
Low	47% (N = 57)	23% (N = 70)	X^2 (1 df) = 8.4, $p < .005$

SOURCE: Phillips Cutright, "Nonpartisan Electoral Systems in American Cities," *Comparative Studies in Society and History* (January 1963), p. 222. Reprinted by permission.

Midwest, unpopular in the South, and even less popular in the West. The distribution is similar for type of ballot [i.e., partisan]," while regional variations in type of election district are much smaller.[43] In addition, the relationship between population mobility and governmental form differs by region, as does the relationship between religious diversity and form. "Although the proportion of children in private school . . . is closely related to form of government, this association is reduced when . . . examined within regions."[44]

Data on suburban governments also show regional variations. The mayoral form predominates in Northeastern and Northcentral locations whereas managers are more common in the West and in the South.[45]

Wolfinger and Field argue that region is a more important determinant of urban political forms than ethnicity. Their data indicate that when governmental forms are examined within regions, this control eliminates most of the ethnic population–unreformed institutions link observed when all cities are examined together, disregarding region. On the other hand, Gordon's study of the relationship of ethnicity to

[43] Wolfinger and Field, "Political Ethos and City Government," pp. 316–17.

[44] Alford and Scoble, "Characteristics of American Cities," pp. 85–86, 90, and 93.

[45] Schnore and Alford, "Forms of Government," p. 9. See Table 2–3 in this volume.

mayoral government concludes that this association is not destroyed by controls for region. But there are differences by region. Over the period studied (1933–60) the association is strongest in the West and next strongest in the Midwest (see Table 2–2).

How is one to interpret findings showing that the region of the country is related to form of government? Does the fact of regional location explain the differential incidence of the various forms? Is it because of some geographical stimulus that manager governments are found disproportionately in the South and mayoral governments in the Northeast? Probably not. It makes little sense as an explanation to argue that mayors are common in the Northeast because that area happens to be north and east of the nation's center or, alternatively, because it is north of the Mason-Dixon line. To make sense as an explanation, region has to comprehend characteristics other than mere geographical placement. Unfortunately, even if it is true that "one can do a much better job of predicting a city's political forms by knowing what part of the country it is in than by knowing anything about the composition of its population,"[46] one still does not know what there is about region that explains or predicts forms. As an explanatory variable region seems awkward and indefinite because regions vary in so many ways: in demography, economy, culture, history, and politics, to name but a few. Which one—or combination—of these characteristics does region index?

This question is important in developing theories from empirical findings. For example, when Wolfinger and Field look at the relationship between ethnicity and governmental forms and control for region, they are subject to the criticism that they have correlated ethnicity with form and then controlled (in part) for ethnicity itself, since ethnicity is one of the demographic characteristics by which regions vary.[47] The same problem of interpretation also crops up elsewhere. Data on all cities over 25,000 population show a close association between private school enrollment and the mayoral form, but this association is reduced when examined within regions. What does this reduced association mean?

---

[46] Wolfinger and Field, "Political Ethos and City Government," p. 320.
[47] Lineberry and Fowler make this point. "Reformism and Public Policies," p. 707.

[Does it] mean that the original association of religious diversity with form of government is spurious? Or merely that the region in which a city is located is correlated highly with both the religious composition of a community . . . and its form of government? We do not really know what it means for a city to be located in a given region, aside from historical patterns of growth and development, and possibly the diffusion of political forms from any adjacent and older cities.[48]

Perhaps the most reasonable perspective on region as an explanatory factor is to acknowledge that it is a composite of many specific variables and thus indexes all its component variables. One can say that the term "region" encompasses all of the ways in which sections of the country differ. Region refers, of course, to broad geographical areas, not cities, but it may nonetheless tell us much about the characteristics of the cities located within it. It might also tell us little. Or it may indicate extracommunity forces (regional culture, for example) acting on cities. In any case, when one says that region *explains* local political phenomena, the explanation must be treated as quite unrefined. For explanatory purposes region is of doubtful utility as a substitute for such local variables as ethnicity, population mobility, and economic base. But regional variations ought to be appreciated as added descriptive information about political phenomena. Also they demonstrate that relationships are not universal and cannot therefore be called laws.

Political Correlates

Interest in descriptive information about governmental forms also suggests another set of variables, namely, political ones. To what extent are various political forms found together or correlated with one another? Specifically, are the main items in the reformist program found together? What extracommunity political variables are associated with urban governmental forms, and can such associations be useful in helping to explain the incidence of the various forms?

Research discloses that the main items in the reformist program—a city manager, nonpartisan elections, and at-large constituencies—

---

[48] Alford and Scoble, "Characteristics of American Cities," p. 93.

are commonly found together. Smaller councils are also common where the classic forms exist.[49] Mixed forms frequently occur as well, especially in cities headed by a mayor. The mixture of forms in mayor-administered cities is indicated by the fact that about as many councilmen in such cities are elected from a combination of ward and at-large constituencies as from ward constituencies alone. And about one-quarter of the mayor-administered cities elect their entire council at-large.

The picture that emerges from this evidence is that reformed institutions are widely found together, just as the reformist, good government program requires them to be. The pure reformed city is alive and well. But there are also many hybrids. Manager-run cities are fairly consistent in their adoption of the two other reformist items, while mayor-administered cities are thoroughly mixed. The latter are frequently characterized by nonpartisan elections and at-large constituencies;[50] moreover, a similar pattern prevails in the suburbs.[51]

Are cities that have adopted "classic" reformed institutions more likely than unreformed cities to adopt "the latest" of the reformed institutions—integrative governments? The evidence suggests that they are not. The two types of communities differ little, if at all, in their inclination to embrace the concept of governmental integration.[52]

Cutright takes an entirely different approach to the subject of political correlates of urban political forms. His analysis of conditions associated with nonpartisan electoral systems combines a standard emphasis on community environmental influences with an unusual emphasis on extracommunity political influences. Proceeding on the assumption that the characteristics of a city political system are to some degree shaped by the larger systems of which they are a part, Cutright examines the relationship between the competitiveness of a state's political system and the existence of partisan elections in that

---

[49] Although based on 1930 figures, these data have very broad implications. See the earlier section on ethnicity and Gordon, "Immigrants and Governmental Form," pp. 161 and 162.

[50] Wolfinger and Field, "Political Ethos and City Government," pp. 312–14.

[51] Schnore and Alford, "Forms of Government," p. 11.

[52] Brett W. Hawkins, "A Note on Urban Political Structure, Environment, and Political Integration," *Polity* (Fall 1969), pp. 32–48.

state's cities. He also examines the relationship of the party loyalty of state voters to local election systems. His data indicate that the two types of cities (those with partisan elections and those with nonpartisan elections) vary importantly in the degree of state party competitiveness and partly loyalty associated with them.[53] Cities with partisan election systems are predominantly found in competitive and high loyalty states. In interpreting these relationships, Cutright considers the characteristics of states in which manager governments and accompanying nonpartisan elections first appeared. Because they were mostly one-party states and because of other relationships observed in his data, he concludes that one-party state environments are conducive to the adoption of nonpartisan elections.

Additional evidence of the impact on cities of state political system characteristics comes from Cutright's analysis of the relationship of community influences to electoral systems. His data indicate that the degree of statewide party competition conditions this relationship.[54] In competitive states measures of community religious and class cleavages discriminate between cities that have adopted and those that have failed to adopt nonpartisan elections, but in one-party states community cleavages have no such impact.

Cutright's data also indicate that weak party loyalty makes an independent contribution to the existence of nonpartisan elections.[55] For example, in one-party Republican states the added factor of low voter loyalty is overwhelmingly associated with nonpartisan elections. In one-party Republican states characterized by low voter loyalty, only one of forty-three cities has retained partisan elections.[56]

For our own purposes, Cutright's analysis is important because it explores in depth the impact of statewide political forms and dispositions on city political system characteristics. Rarely has the influence of extracommunity political variables been analyzed so systematically or on such a comparative scale as in Cutright's study of nonpartisan elections. Nor has there often been such a clear-cut statement of the

---

[53] Party loyalty is crudely measured by the average of the third-party vote in the 1912 and 1924 presidential elections.
[54] Cutright, "Nonpartisan Electoral Systems," p. 313.
[55] *Ibid.*
[56] *Ibid.*, pp. 304–305.

importance of extracommunity variables in explaining urban governmental forms.

Correlates of Governmental Fragmentation and Integration

A new wrinkle has in recent years been added to the reformers' traditional plea for efficiency and economy in government. Not satisfied with merely bemoaning partisan politics and the absence of professional administrators, reformers now also complain about governmental fragmentation. Believing that "too many governments" infest the nation's urban areas, reformers charge that this "multiplicity" of governments encourages inefficient administration, duplicated governmental functions, and reduced ability to cope with problems that cross jurisdictional boundaries. In short, they believe that such fragmentation adversely affects governmental performance. Nor are reformers reluctant to offer their solutions to the problem. On the contrary, they have put forth a great many inventive proposals in the form of devices to integrate or to centralize urban governments. The forms of integration suggested include city-county consolidation, intermunicipal consolidation, annexation, metropolitan special districts, and an urban or municipalized county (which involves granting municipal-like powers to a county).

What conditions are associated with fragmented governmental structures in the metropolis? What conditions are associated with the successful adoption of integrative governments? What environmental characteristics are conducive to political integration? And what do we know about voter and group inputs concerning political integration?

Fragmentation[57]

To date neither reformers nor their critics have made much effort to measure comparatively the extent of "fragmentation" in each of the nation's metropolitan areas (although the Bureau of the Census has).

[57] This section is based on Brett W. Hawkins and Thomas R. Dye, "Metropolitan 'Fragmentation': A Research Note," *Midwest Review of Public Administration* (February 1970), pp. 17–24.

The concept of metropolitan fragmentation can be operationally measured by specifying either the number of governmental units in a metropolitan area (an absolute measure of fragmentation) or the number of governmental units *per person* (a relative measure of fragmentation). In 1967 the number of governments operating in the nation's 277 metropolitan areas was 20,703 (a figure equal to 25 percent of the number of local governments in the entire United States). This figure included 5,018 school districts, 4,977 municipalities, 3,255 townships, 404 counties, and 7,049 special districts. In 1967 there was one governmental unit for approximately every 5,600 persons living in metropolitan areas and one for every 940 persons living elsewhere. Thus, on the whole metropolitan areas are considerably *less* fragmented than nonmetropolitan areas—a fact that may help to explain the rising demands for governmental decentralization, neighborhood autonomy, and increased citizen participation in the metropolis.

Individual metropolitan areas differ widely in the complexity of their governmental forms. According to the 1967 census of governments the Chicago metropolitan area has the most fragmented governmental system in the nation. A total of 1,113 local governments operate in this area, including 327 school districts, 6 counties, 250 municipalities, 113 townships, and 417 special districts. Other metropolitan areas with complex governmental structures include Philadelphia with 876 governments, Pittsburgh with 704, New York with 551, St. Louis with 474, Portland with 385, San Francisco with 312, and Los Angeles with 233. In contrast, there are several single-county metropolitan areas (mainly in the South) with fewer than 10 governmental units.

Governmental fragmentation in metropolitan areas is a function of size: the larger the metropolitan area, the more fragmented the governmental structure. The simple coefficients in Table 2–7 indicate that about 50 percent of the variation in the number of governments in metropolitan areas can be attributed to size. Fragmentation is also related to age of settlement and to income levels in the metropolis, although these factors are less influential than size. Apparently, the older a metropolitan area is, the more complex its governmental structure; moreover, the more affluent its citizens, the more complexity (in the form of separate, relatively small units of government) they can afford. Further analysis indicates that age and income are *independently*

Table 2–7 Conditions Associated with Metropolitan Governmental Fragmentation

	Numbers of Governments			Governments per 100,000 Population		
	Total	School Districts	Municipalities	Total	School Districts	Municipalities
Size of metropolitan area	.71	.67	.74	−.15	−.11	.00
Age in decades	.48	.40	.49	−.19	−.14	.00
Percentage nonwhite, central city	.06	.00	−.04	−.37	−.31	−.03
Metropolitan-wide SES[a]						
Median family income	.28	.29	.24	.00	.00	−.05
White collar occupation	.15	.14	.15	.03	−.07	.07
High school graduate	.06	.08	.01	.12	.06	.08
City-Suburban SES[a] Differences						
Nonwhite	.05	.01	.17	−.22	−.17	−.03
Median family income	.15	.07	.24	−.16	−.21	.00
White collar occupation	.17	.11	.26	−.26	−.25	−.04
High school graduate	.22	.16	.27	−.11	−.17	.00
Central city population as percentage of SMSA[b] population	−.23	−.19	−.27	.14	.09	.05

NOTE: Figures are simple correlation coefficients for 212 metropolitan areas.
[a] Socioeconomic status.
[b] Standard Metropolitan Statistical Area.

SOURCE: Brett W. Hawkins and Thomas R. Dye, "Metropolitan 'Fragmentation': A Research Note," *Midwest Review of Public Administration* (February 1970), p. 19. Reprinted by permission.

(though weakly) related to fragmentation. These relationships are not a product of the intervening effect of size.

Contrary to expectations, the racial composition of the central city does not correlate with fragmentation. One might expect that increases in the central city's nonwhite population would be associated with "white flight" to the suburbs and the development and incorporation of independent suburbs—thus, with fragmentation. But the data do not support this theory. One might also expect that city-suburban differences in socioeconomic levels would be related to fragmentation. Again, this expectation is based on a belief that middle class whites seeking to escape from the problems of less affluent central city populations would develop and incorporate independent suburbs, thereby contributing to fragmentation. But the relationships between city-suburban social differences and fragmentation are generally so weak (i.e., the coefficients so low) that this does not appear to be an explanation of fragmentation (see Table 2–7).

Finally, we should note that central city dominance of the metropolitan area, as indexed by the percentage of the metropolitan population living in the central city, is inversely related to fragmentation. Governmental fragmentation is less in central cities that have managed to hold on to a substantial proportion of the metropolitan population.

If fragmentation is measured in *relative* terms (number of governments per 100,000 residents), it becomes more difficult to detect environmental correlates. Governmental complexity in relative terms is *not* associated with size. In fact, there is a slight tendency for larger, older, and racially heterogeneous metropolitan areas to have *fewer* governments per capita.

Integration

In a study of annexation in 213 urbanized areas, Thomas R. Dye discovered several important social and political correlates of integration. Legal restraints imposed by state law, he found, are related to success of annexation; that is, annexation increases with increasing statutory permissiveness—but not uniformly so. While statutory permissiveness does not by itself satisfactorily explain success in annexation, Dye's focus on this variable is nonetheless of special interest (in terms of the theoretical framework of this book) because legal restraints under state law can be regarded as *extracommunity political variables*. However, Dye finds a *community political variable* more closely related to annexation activity. In fact, form of government emerges as one of the most important explanatory variables in the annexation study. Manager governments are significantly more likely to engage in annexation than nonmanager governments. And this association persists even under controls for population size, age of city settlement, status characteristics of the city population, and city-fringe social differences. Why might this be so? Assuming that people believe manager governments to be "nonpolitical" and "efficient," we might expect manager-led cities to encounter less opposition to their annexation efforts in the territories to be annexed than would cities with a "politicized" executive.[58]

Age of settlement also emerges as an important explanatory variable in the annexation study. Of course, one might expect older cities to have populations quite different from those of their fringes; and although this is true it does not explain the association between age of settlement and annexation. What does explain it? Dye speculates that through the years people and organizations may adjust themselves to boundaries as they find them. Inertia may set in to resist change.[59] The size of the area's population, on the other hand, is not closely related to annexation activity: "central cities in smaller urbanized areas had only slightly more success in annexing people than cities in larger urbanized areas."[60]

Dye also examines the status characteristics of central cities and the difference in status between cities and fringes for their relation to annexation success. Cities with more "middle class" educational and occupational attributes are more likely to annex surrounding territories. More important than city characteristics, however, is the differential in status between cities and their suburbs. Differences favoring the suburbs emerge as a distinct barrier to political integration. And they remain important even when the effects of population size, age of settlement, and form of government are controlled.[61] The

---

[58] Thomas R. Dye, "Urban Political Integration: Conditions Associated with Annexation in American Cities," *Midwest Journal of Political Science* (November 1964), pp. 435–36.
[59] *Ibid.*, pp. 436 and 446.
[60] *Ibid.*, p. 445.
[61] *Ibid.*, p. 443.

explanation of the association seems to be that suburbanites who are very different from their "city neighbors" see political integration as social integration with undesirables, or at least with people whose values and life styles they do not share. Where suburbanites are not very different from their city neighbors, this barrier is missing. Although no direct evidence of differences in values between demographically different city and fringe residents is available, these values are reasonable explanations for the close associations in Dye's data. And they crop up elsewhere in the literature on the conditions of urban political integration.

Successful adoption of integrative governments is also the subject of a comparative study by Brett W. Hawkins. Whereas Dye operationally equates political integration with annexation, Hawkins defines it in terms of several other integrative devices, including consolidation, federation, the municipalized county, and area-wide special districts. The author studies forty-one referenda on these devices, attempting to determine whether community political variables are more closely related to referendum success than environmental variables. Indicators of reformed and unreformed institutions are examined for their relationship with successful referenda, as are state legal requirements and indicators of the partisan competitiveness of each urban area's state environment.

Among the political variables (both community and extracommunity types) only legal requirements are importantly related to outcome. Less restrictive requirements are closely associated with success. On the other hand, a less competitive state party environment is not associated with success. Nor are reformed political institutions, even though one might expect that communities that have already adopted "classic" reformed institutions would also tend to adopt the latest reformed institution. Finally, the data do not indicate that approval by the suburbs is more likely when the city proposing integration has "professionalized, efficient" institutions. Suburban approval is thoroughly scattered among reformed and unreformed city governments.

On the other hand, environmental variables are closely related to political integration. Indicators of human, economic, and spatial diversity in the urban community are negatively related to success.[62] This

[62] See Hawkins, "Note on Urban Political Structure."

finding suggests that integration is least likely where there is great subcommunity, interest group, and value diversity. Such diversity appears to index greater conflict over politics. The reader will recall that Cutright found indicators of community cleavage similarly discriminating between cities that adopted and failed to adopt nonpartisan elections. Kessel found socioeconomic variables similarly discriminating between cities adopting mayoral and manager forms; and Schnore and Alford found suburban social structure similarly discriminating between suburban communities adopting manager and mayoral forms. The integration study thus adds to the accumulating evidence of the political impact of urban social diversity.

Like studies of classic reformed institutions, in other words, studies posing questions about conditions associated with integrative governments turn up answers that emphasize social differentiation. In both cases greater differentiation is associated with the failure of reform efforts. Additional support for this generalization comes from a study of intermunicipal cooperation in the Philadelphia metropolitan area[63] in which the researchers attempt to analyze the effect of urban differentiation on cooperative, or integrative, arrangements between contiguous municipalities. Their central hypothesis is that agreements will occur more frequently among communities that are similar in social, economic, and political characteristics. Data on cooperation concerning public schools support the hypothesis; that is, there are smaller differences among cooperating than noncooperating pairs in social rank, community wealth, and Republican voting. Overall there is a pattern of findings in the Philadelphia area that supports the hypothesis that intermunicipal cooperation is a function of social, economic, and political distance. "These findings suggest that social and economic differentiation among urban communities may be fundamental to the whole question of metropolitan government. The highly differentiated character of metropolitan communities may operate to maintain our present fragmented structure of local government and to inhibit the growth of inter-governmental cooperation."[64]

---

[63] Thomas R. Dye *et al.*, "Differentiation and Cooperation in a Metropolitan Area," *Midwest Journal of Political Science* (May 1963), pp. 145–55.

[64] *Ibid.*, p. 155. Henry Teune cites a similar study done by one of his students, also in the Philadelphia area, that found no significant differences between com-

Another generalization about intergovernmental cooperation, the "spill-over" theory, suggests that once one agreement is made others tend to follow—as a result of learned integrative habits culminating in further integration. Spill-over theory holds that integrative behavior is usually generalized from one governmental function to another, often resulting eventually in the outright merger of communities. Counter to the theory, we find that intergovernmental agreements in Philadelphia are not concentrated among governments with a large number of agreements. However, the Philadelphia data include no assessment of whether previous agreements were rewarding or punishing. Spill-over theory does not suggest that unrewarding integrative experiences will lead to further integration.[65]

Also supporting generalizations linking environmental variables (i.e., indicators of diversity or conflict in the urban environment) with the failure of political integration is Henry J. Schmandt's study of Milwaukee and its suburbs.[66] As already shown, however, the relationship of *political* variables to integration is less patterned. Conflicting evidence abounds. On the one hand, annexation is associated with manager government and less restrictive state laws, and intermunicipal cooperation concerning schools is associated with Republican voting. On the other hand, Hawkins' study of several types of integration finds almost no correlation with political variables (legal requirements of the referendum being the sole exception). The idea of a link between classic reformist political institutions and political integration has intuitive appeal in that one might expect suburbanites to agree to merge with cities run in an "efficient" and "professionalized" manner. Also, one might expect communities that have adopted the classic reforms to be places where widely shared values favor the efficient provision of public services. Since these values led to reformed institutions in the

---

munities with similar status and voting patterns—except in school agreements. See "The Learning of Integrative Habits," in *The Integration of Political Communities,* eds. Carl Deutsch *et al.* (Philadelphia: Lippincott, 1964), pp. 264 and 265.

[65] Deutsch *et al., The Integration of Political Communities,* pp. 260–61.

[66] See Henry J. Schmandt, "The City and the Ring: The Two-Way Street of Metropolitan Reorganization," *American Behavioral Scientist* (November 1960), pp. 17–19.

past, they could be expected to do so in the future. Unfortunately, we can find no data from public opinion surveys showing that suburban residents who accepted integration proposals in fact perceived city governments having reformed institutions to be economical, efficient, or professionalized. The available aggregate data, moreover, do not all point in the same direction. Thus, confident generalizations about the relationship of political variables to metropolitan integration still elude political scientists.

Why Republican voting should be related to intermunicipal cooperation is hard to see and is not explained in the Philadelphia study. It may reflect the explanatory power of an environmental variable closely related to both Republican voting and political integration, namely, higher class standing.

Interestingly, studies of voter and group support of political integration indirectly offer evidence about the generation of demands in urban environments. Little is known about the way in which demands arise, are transmitted to city political systems, and affect the structural characteristics of city systems. In the governmental reorganization literature, however, there is some evidence regarding factors that stimulate demand inputs. The literature tells us something about conditions associated with voter and group support of reorganization. For example, data on charter reform proposals in twenty-two Pennsylvania cities show three political process variables (fear of higher costs as an issue, type of reform proposal, and voter turnout in the referendum) and one environmental variable (population size) to be correlated with the "yes" vote. Class and social heterogeneity indicators are not correlated with support.[67] Other studies show that certain community values are related to support of political integration, that is, to inputs favoring a change in structure. For example, "cosmopolitan" attitudes are related to support of integration.[68] Similarly, persons who are not anomic tend to support integration.[69] These two conclusions are based

---

[67] Clarke, "Environment, Process and Policy," p. 1180.

[68] Thomas R. Dye, "The Local-Cosmopolitan Dimension and the Study of Urban Politics," *Social Forces* (March 1963), p. 244.

[69] See Edward L. McDill and Jeanne Claire Ridley, "Status, Anomia, Political Alienation, and Political Participation," *American Journal of Sociology* (September 1962), pp. 205–13.

on data in single metropolitan areas, Philadelphia and Nashville respectively. But they suggest theoretically interesting relationships between individual social-psychological attributes and the generation of support for urban political integration.

A large body of evidence, including data from Nashville, St. Louis, and Cleveland,[70] supports the linking of higher class status with support of integrative governments. Other variables shown to be importantly associated with support of integrative governments in single-city studies are dissatisfaction with public services (Nashville, 1962), central city residence,[71] suburban suspicion of the central city (Nashville, 1962), urbanlike values[72] among suburbanites (Nashville, 1958), residence in larger and more dense communities (Cleveland), and a nonindustrial economic base (Cleveland).

More evidence of conditions of support comes from two comparative studies. In an analysis of support of city-county consolidation, measures of a familistic way of life were positively related to the yes vote. (A "familistic way of life" places a high value on the family, its living space, and amenities that improve family life.) In addition, both city and fringe social rank were positively correlated with support. Surprisingly, social differences in favor of the fringe were *positively* re-

[70] Brett W. Hawkins, "Public Opinion and Metropolitan Reorganization in Nashville," *Journal of Politics* (May 1966), pp. 408–18; Scott Greer, *Metropolitics: A Study of Political Culture* (New York: Wiley, 1963); and Richard A. Watson and John Romani, "Metropolitan Cleveland: An Analysis of the Voting Record," *Midwest Journal of Political Science* (November 1961), pp. 382–84. See also David A. Booth, *Metro Politics: The Nashville Consolidation* (East Lansing, Michigan: Institute for Community Development and Services of Michigan State University, 1963), Chapter 3, which shows a similar relationship in the 1958 defeat of city-county consolidation in Nashville and Davidson County, Tennessee.

[71] A common pattern in reorganization referenda has been a favorable vote in the city and an unfavorable vote outside the city. This occurred in Athens-Clarke County, Georgia, in 1969, in the Louisville area in 1956, in the Macon area in 1960, in the Nashville area in 1958, and in the Richmond area in 1961.

[72] Measured by responses to a question asking people to choose from a list of considerations they used in deciding to live in a particular suburban neighborhood. Selection of the responses "closeness to big stores, to work, and to professional services" and "good municipal services, e.g., sewers, sidewalks, police and firemen" were treated as indicating urbanlike values. See Booth, *Metro Politics*, p. 43.

lated to fringe support. In a wider study of forty-two efforts to reorganize metropolitan area governments, the same positive relationship between social differences in favor of the fringe and fringe support was found. Both studies suggest that as life style differences increasingly favor the fringe there is an increasing tendency for fringe voters to vote *for,* not against, political integration. This finding holds, moreover, in both large and small cities, in successful and unsuccessful referenda, in the South and outside the South, and whether or not the proposals involve the elimination of a unit of government.[73]

Both theory and research suggest that substantially different kinds of people are unlikely to merge and form new communities. Of course, fringe-city differences in styles of life are thought to be an especially important type of difference among urbanites. Why, then, should life style differences in the fringes' favor be positively related to fringe support of political integration? These data indirectly conflict (the data describe voter support, not referendum outcome) with Dye's finding that fringe-city differences are associated with less annexation activity by cities and with Hawkins' finding that urban area (not fringe-city) differentiation is negatively related to the passage of referenda on integrative governments.[74] One explanation of this deviant finding is that residents of the fringes of the particular cities studied may want better public services and support political integration as a way to get them. The idea is that familistic, child-oriented fringe electorates see integrative governments as a way to get services that enhance and preserve their familistic way of life (or at least help them to get services they want, whether for familistic reasons or not). If this is true, their support of political integration is a pro- not an anti-life style phenomenon.

In any case, this study challenges the idea that social heterogeneity necessarily leads to negative inputs concerning political integration. Life style differences between fringes and cities are associated with

---

[73] Brett W. Hawkins, "Life Style, Demographic Distance, and Voter Support of City-County Consolidation," *Social Science Quarterly* (December 1967), pp. 325–37, and Hawkins, "Fringe-City Life Style Distance and Fringe Support of Political Integration," *American Journal of Sociology* (November 1968), pp. 248–55.

[74] Hawkins, "Note on Urban Political Structure."

fringe *support,* not opposition, to political integration. These data suggest that fringe-city life style differences are not the generalized obstacle to political integration that many students have thought them to be. In fact, the data indicate that such differences may spur a yes vote, at least where high rates of growth have taken place. There may be more important types of urban differentiation than that between cities and fringes, at least insofar as political integration is concerned.

In addition to providing evidence of voter support of integrative governments, studies show that organized groups perceive integrative governments as either harmful or advantageous and activate themselves accordingly. Support comes from metropolitan newspapers, leagues of women voters, central city chambers of commerce, commercial and real estate interests, central city officials, and academic spokesmen. On the other hand, county government employees, residents of rural areas, and employees of suburban governments tend to oppose integrative efforts. Evidence of these patterns is available in case studies of St. Louis, Cleveland, Miami, and Nashville, and in a multi-city survey by the United States Advisory Commission on Inter-governmental Relations.[75]

Conclusions

What valid generalizations can we derive from the various studies of the environmental base of urban governmental forms? Unfortunately, we can derive few to which there is no exception. However, we can call attention to patterns of relationships. Clearly the most frequent pattern relates to the political impact of social differences among people. Indicators of ethnic, religious, and life style differences are associated with the retention of unreformed, politicized, group arbitrating forms—including decentralized, fragmented governments. The same is true where the local economy, subcommunities, population size, and population stability suggest more human diversity and a cementing of people's socioeconomic ties to the community. Lesser differences are associated with the adoption of reformed

---

[75] *Factors Affecting Voter Reactions to Governmental Reorganization in Metropolitan Areas* (Washington, D. C.: Government Printing Office, 1962).

institutions.[76] All of these relationships suggest that the more stable the social heterogeneity of the urban population the greater the pressures generated for institutions that are better at giving political access to community groups. Alford and Scoble sum up the pattern as follows:

> Social heterogeneity—the existence of sizeable groups with diverse political cultures and demands—favors a more "politicized," less centralized, less professionalized form because there is not as great a consensus among politically active groups upon the proper goals of city government and a greater need for access and representation from diverse groups.[77]

Charles S. Liebman puts it this way:

> From our knowledge of political behavior in general we assume (a) that different socioeconomic characteristics imply different kinds of politically oriented groups and different relationships of dominance between politically oriented groups; from this we infer (b) that the presence of different kinds of groups and the dominance of different groups as measured by their quantitative relationship to one another leads to different outcomes; from this in turn we infer (c) that some of these outcomes relate to the structure and institutions of government . . .[78]

The evidence suggests that the insights of James Madison and Karl Marx apply very well to the modern urban world. Social and economic differences appear to be at the base of political differences relating to governmental structure. Socioeconomic diversity suggests that people have competing goals for government and that they engage in conflict over these goals. Of course, the literature contains little direct evidence of goals, but the pattern of evidence is logically ex-

[76] Analysis of communities abandoning the manager plan shows them to be consistently deviant demographically from the ideal type manager community. Abandonments evidently are probable where the local population is relatively less prosperous, mobile, and homogeneous with respect to religion and ethnicity. Robert L. Bray, "Political and Socioeconomic Characteristics of Council-Manager Abandonments" (Seminar paper, Department of Political Science, University of Georgia, August 1969).

[77] Alford and Scoble, "Characteristics of American Cities," p. 83.

[78] Liebman, "Functional Differentiation and Political Characteristics," p. 489.

plained with the following linked theory: different environmental characteristics imply different groups' having some conflicting political goals; these conflicting goals are transmitted to the urban political system and have an effect on the characteristics of that system. Policy is related to group conflict which is related to socioeconomic diversity. As Liebman correctly points out, this theory is supported by other knowledge about political behavior. Political scientists have long been interested in the "social anchorage" of political opinion and behavior, i.e., in the relationship of nonpolitical groups to political behavior. A considerable literature indicates that social group membership or identification affects voting and opinion. This "social determinism" seems to be based on interaction by group members, psychological identification with the group, and distinctive stimuli felt by group members as compared with others. In this literature, too, the main idea is that different social groupings generate different, sometimes conflicting, demands; when these demands are sufficiently potent, government responds.

Caution is in order, however. In the first place, the associations reported in the literature are not so close as to demonstrate that one can accurately predict governmental forms simply by knowing the characteristics of the environment. Much of the variation in governmental forms remains unexplained (i.e., unassociated with variables). Even more basically, it is doubtful that correlations between environmental variables and forms of government constitute adequate explanations in terms of the theories that the correlations suggest. To provide explanations with the data used researchers must resort to concepts not really measured but only indirectly suggested by observed relationships, such as "socially differentiated demands on government" or "political conflict." The implicit assumption in most of this research is that numbers (or proportions) of certain groups of people index that group's political goals, preferences, dominance, or policy influence.[79] In fact, this assumption remains untested.

We do not have much direct evidence about the city-relevant political goals of the groups in question or their demand activities. The studies cited here, with few exceptions, do not directly measure goals, preferences, or demands (inputs). Instead, they measure socio-

---

[79] Lineberry and Fowler, "Reformism and Public Policies," p. 707.

economic diversity and postulate that diversity indicates social cleavage, political conflict, competing interests, or socially differentiated demands concerning political institutions. The degree to which this is true is unknown. Taking this fact into account, it is reasonable to argue that, while it is useful to know how the environmental attributes of reformed and unreformed cities differ (since these differences suggest explanations), such classifications do not in themselves constitute full explanations.[80] There is almost no reliable evidence of the way in which environmental characteristics are related to the generation of socially differentiated demands relevant to structure. Although it appears that urbanites perceive some institutional arrangements as functioning to their advantage and some to their disadvantage (by the differential way institutions grant access to community groups, for example), this is based more on inference than direct evidence. And although political scientists have discovered many theoretically interesting correlates of urban political forms, we know little about how demands arise in the urban community, are then transmitted to the system, and influence the system's structure. To this extent our explanations of structures are incomplete. We have yet to describe in much detail—much less account for or measure the impact of—policy-relevant interactions between urban populations and governments.

Still another criticism of this literature is that it represents the continued influence on urban political research of reformist concepts —the correlates of "reformed" and "unreformed" governments—when emphasis might more usefully be placed on dynamic concerns (for example, on the sequence of political events leading up to policy outputs).[81]

It is also important to consider the fact that some studies contradict, or at least qualify, theory linking urban social diversity with unreformed institutions. Many studies find little social disparity between reformed and unreformed cities; another indicates that, contrary to expectations, life style diversity between the city and the fringe is not associated with fringe opposition to political integrative governments.

---

[80] Bryan T. Downes and Timothy M. Hennessey, "Theory and Concept Formation in Problems of Process and Change" (Paper delivered at the 1969 meeting of the American Political Science Association, New York), Part I, p. 12.

[81] *Ibid.,* Part I, abstract and p. 1.

Clearly many factors besides "environmental conduciveness" in the form of ethnic, religious, class, and economic base differences can and do shape political institutions. These may include local disasters, scandals, and the special goals of elites (as opposed to broad population groupings).

chapter 3
Community Environment and Urban Policies

The time-honored practice of explaining policy by examining only actions within the political system—whether performed by expressly political actors or not—has lost status among political scientists. Such aspects of formal political power as official leadership positions, governmental structure, and the attributes of officials have lost some of their former standing as explanatory variables. Accompanying this demotion of system variables, however, has been a greater emphasis on environmental variables. Many recent studies of state and local policy outputs as well as earlier studies of community decision making suggest that policies are more a product of environmental than system factors and that environment can only be ignored at the cost of adequate explanation. Recent studies imply that political scientists have been too preoccupied with system variables and that a theoretical widening is needed to take into account the explanatory power of environments. Environmental variables are more important than system variables, or at least as important, in explaining policy.[1]

[1] See Thomas R. Dye, *Politics, Economics, and the Public* (Chicago: Rand McNally, 1966), p. 299, and Richard I. Hofferbert, "Elite Influence in Policy Formation: A Model for Comparative Inquiry" (Paper delivered at the 1968 meeting of the American Political Science Association, Washington, D.C.).

The elitist stream of the community power literature reveals the policy importance of unofficial, extragovernmental elites. On "key" issues (if not routine ones) a relatively few individuals not having formally recognized authority in fact exert disproportionate, even determinative, influence. The degree to which this outside elite is monolithic is subject to dispute, as is the role of economic resources in determining an elite's influence; but the fact of outside influence over policy emerges clearly from all elitist studies. Private persons having no official power at all are nonetheless powerful, and their power is often generalized across several policy (issue) areas.[2]

Although not noticeably grateful, political scientists are indebted to their sociologist colleagues for calling attention to the impact of unofficial elites on community policy. The main stimulus to this area of research was Floyd Hunter's study of Atlanta.[3] Hunter found a pyramid-shaped structure of power with a relatively few "top leaders" being decisively influential in important community-wide decisions.[4] These "top leaders" consisted primarily of commercial, financial, and industrial elites, but a few governmental officials were also represented.

Hunter allowed his sample of leaders to designate the issues that they thought were of major importance to Atlanta; he then found these

---

[2] The studies cited in this section concern the policy consequences of different power structures, especially those that are highly centralized outside of government. In other words, power structure is treated as an independent variable. The reader should also be aware of studies treating power structure as the dependent variable (the one to be explained). Recent comparative studies in this vein are of special interest. They include: John Walton, "Substance and Artifact: The Current Status of Research on Community Power Structure," *American Journal of Sociology* (January 1966), pp. 430–38; Walton, "The Vertical Axis of Community Organization and the Structure of Power," *Southwestern Social Science Quarterly* (December 1967), pp. 353–68; Claire W. Gilbert, "Some Trends in Community Politics: A Secondary Analysis of Power Structure Data from 166 Communities," *Southwestern Social Science Quarterly* (December 1967), pp. 373–81; and Terry N. Clark, "Community Structure, Decision-Making, Budget Expenditures and Urban Renewal in 51 American Communities," *American Sociological Review* (August 1968), pp. 585–87. The last study treats power structure as both an independent and a dependent variable.

[3] Floyd Hunter, *Community Power Structure: A Study of Decision Makers* (Chapel Hill: University of North Carolina Press, 1954).

[4] *Ibid.*, p. 62.

leaders to be instrumental in determining the outcome of these issues.[5] Despite this and other weaknesses in his methodology, results similar to Hunter's have been found in studies of many communities, often with due consideration given to reputed influentials' activities on specific issues (i.e., not just reputation but activities were scrutinized). Domination of decisions by a small group of economic leaders was found in "community A" in 1954 and again in 1961.[6] In another study a Chicago urban renewal project succeeded largely because of the organization of a citizens' group in the renewal area.[7] A study of the elites of Atlanta subsequent to Hunter's qualified his conclusions about that city (finding less generalized power among the reputed elite and concluding that those occupying major economic positions were not of major importance in the outcome of the five issues studied), but the later study showed that persons outside of government perceived to be most influential actually did engage in actions that showed them, in fact, to be influential.[8]

An effort to predict the outcome of two constitutional amendments in Denver was successful, and "top influential solidarity and activity" was a key component of the prediction model.[9] A study of policy-making leaders in one American and one English city found no single, solidary elite; but it did discern an important impact by extra-governmental influentials.[10] In two upstate New York communities Robert Presthus found two distinct decision-making systems, one po-

[5] See Ernest A. T. Barth and Stuart D. Johnson, "Community Power and a Typology of Social Issues," *Social Forces* (October 1959), pp. 29–32.

[6] George Belknap and Ralph Schmuckler, "Political Power Relations in a Midwest City," *Public Opinion Quarterly* (Spring 1956), pp. 73–81, and David A. Booth and Charles R. Adrian, "Power Structure and Community Change: A Replication Study of Community A," *Midwest Journal of Political Science* (August 1962), pp. 277–96.

[7] Peter H. Rossi and Robert A. Dentler, *The Politics of Urban Renewal* (New York: Free Press, 1961).

[8] M. Kent Jennings, *Community Influentials* (New York: Free Press, 1962), p. 199.

[9] Robert C. Hanson, "Predicting a Community Decision: A Test of the Miller-Form Theory," *American Sociological Review* (October 1959), pp. 662–71.

[10] Delbert C. Miller, "Decision-Making Cliques in Community Power Structures: A Comparative Study of an American and an English City, *American Journal of Sociology* (November 1958), pp. 299–310.

litical and the other economic. Economic leaders whose power rested on their social status and positions in industry, finance, and business dominated community decisions not requiring the use of public funds.[11]

In a much-respected study of four communities, Robert E. Agger, Daniel Goldrich, and Bert E. Swanson discovered narrow distributions of power. Even in those communities classified as having "mass" power structures, "there were ordinarily narrow or elite distributions of political power in most decisional processes."[12] The "mass" classification emerged because relative standards were used in data analysis; that is, a community's power structure was classified as mass when the distribution of power in one or more of its decision-making processes was broader than for any of the processes in another community.[13] A study of six American and two Mexican communities in the Southwest discerned a stratified structure of influence, with businessmen most often represented.[14] Another study of six Southwestern cities concluded—after studying "the actual exercise of power in a broad range of community decisions"—that reputed general influentials were in fact deeply involved in community decision making.[15] In other words, influentials according to general reputation were found to be influenced on concrete issues.

Evidence that reputed influentials are in fact influential also appeared in a recent study of eighteen New England communities. When reputational leaders were both active and united, they were on the winning side of an issue three-fourths of the time (fifty-four out of

[11] Robert Presthus, *Men at the Top* (New York: Oxford University Press, 1964), pp. 405–406.

[12] Robert E. Agger, Daniel Goldrich, and Bert E. Swanson, *The Rulers and the Ruled* (New York: Wiley, 1964), p. 75.

[13] *Ibid*.

[14] William V. D'Antonio *et al.*, "Institutional and Occupational Representations in Eleven Community Influence Systems, *American Sociological Review* (June 1961), pp. 440–46. The figure "eleven" stems from the fact that eight communities studied are compared with three others for which data are available from the published literature. Data on all eleven communities point to the same conclusion.

[15] William V. D'Antonio and Eugene C. Erickson, "The Reputational Technique as a Measure of Community Power: An Evaluation Based on Comparative and Longitudinal Studies," *American Sociological Review* (June 1966), pp. 362–76.

seventy-two issues). More importantly, they had as high a proportion of wins when they supported the *less active* side.[16] Nor were reputational leaders associated with successful outcomes simply because they supported the status quo; on the contrary, they achieved their greatest success against the status quo. The author of the New England study concluded that reputation is a usable power resource in much the same way that wealth, social standing, or authority might be. Reputation is a "stable and generalized persuasion resource," and because it is there is reality to the reputation for influence.[17]

A study of small hospital projects in 218 communities also provides evidence of the influence of extragovernmental elites—especially in the Northeast. Taking projects in all regions together, businessmen, professionals, and executives made up more than three-fourths of the most active persons. Government officials made up only 8.2 percent; and in the Northeast none of the highest ranked decision makers was an officeholder or political leader. Decision making in the Northeast rests in persons of property and general influence.[18]

The point of this discussion of elitist findings about community power centers on the policy influence of persons outside of government. Elitist findings reveal the significant impact of factors outside the political system and the limitations of official political behavior. In this sense it is not really crucial whether power structures are highly centralized, only somewhat centralized, or quite competitive—or even whether persons with the most political influence have the most economic resources under their control. What counts is that the influence originates outside the political system and is unofficial.

Population Variables

The importance of environmental influences on city policy is underscored by many comparative studies of taxes and spending. Studies of

[16] William A. Gamson, "Reputation and Resources in Community Politics," *American Journal of Sociology* (September 1966), pp. 121–31.

[17] *Ibid.*, pp. 122, 124, and 131.

[18] Paul A. Miller, "The Process of Decision-Making Within the Context of Community Organization," *Rural Sociology* (March 1952), pp. 153–61.

general taxes and expenditures avoid the narrowness of studies dealing only with controversial issues; moreover, the former may cover issues of greater concern to the masses than those usually treated in the literature on community power.

Population size, density, distribution, and change—which are treated as indicators of environmental pressures, needs, or demands on government—commonly correlate with city expenditures. Population size is correlated with urban renewal and general budgetary expenditures in fifty-one cities, even when the effect of other variables is taken into account. Tables 3–1 and 3–2 show that, although other characteristics of the urban environment are more important, population size has an independent effect. As size increases, expenditures do likewise,[19] presumably reflecting increased needs and demands for services generated by population growth. Size is also associated with racial segregation in schools. Examination of both pupil and teacher segregation shows that larger cities (especially in the North) are more segregated than smaller ones. One reason may be that larger cities are less amenable to policy change than smaller ones. Larger cities have larger bureaucracies, and large bureaucracies often resist policy change. Increases in population also expand the number of interest groups that may exercise a veto over policy change and increase residential segregation.[20]

On the other hand, population size, density, and growth are not associated with city planning expenditures.[21] Moreover, data on all cities over 25,000 show little or no correlation between general expenditures per capita and city population size.[22]

Variations in spending and taxing among sixty-four metropolitan New York municipalities are more closely related to population size than all other factors combined. Eighty-three percent of the variance

---

[19] Clark, "Community Structure in 51 American Communities," pp. 587–88.

[20] Thomas R. Dye, "Urban School Segregation: A Comparative Analysis," *Urban Affairs Quarterly* (December 1968), pp. 141–65.

[21] Robert Lineberry, "Community Structure and Planning Commitment: A Note on the Correlates of Agency Expenditures," *Social Science Quarterly* (December 1969), Table 1.

[22] Louis A. Froman, "An Analysis of Public Policies in Cities," *Journal of Politics* (February 1967), p. 106.

Table 3–1 Correlations and Path Coefficients
for the Dependent Variable:
Urban Renewal Expenditures

Dependent Variable: Urban Renewal Expenditures

Independent Variable	Zero Order Correlation	Path Coefficient
Catholic population	.454	.620
Community poverty	.136	.527
Population size	.392	.340
Decentralized decision-making structure	.350	.291
Highly educated population	−.297	.282
Economic diversification	.050	−.235
Industrial activity	.119	.181
Index of reform government	−.308	.052
Civic voluntary organization activity	−.051	.025
Residual	—	.708

NOTE: This table gives the correlation of each variable with urban renewal expenditures without controlling for other variables ("Zero Order Correlation") and while controlling for them ("Path Coefficient").

SOURCE: Terry N. Clark, "Community Structure, Decision-Making, Budget Expenditures, and Urban Renewal in 51 American Communities," *American Sociological Review* (August 1968), p. 587. Reprinted by permission of the American Sociological Association.

in expenditures is explained statistically by community size. Thirteen percent is explained by the combination of industrialization, housing density, age, low income population, and residential affluence.[23] Among indicators of pressures or demands from the environment, in other words, population size exerts the most potent influence on spending.

Size is also related to educational policy outcomes in sixty-seven cities (see Table 3–3). While taking into account the effects of other possible influences (such as the educational, occupational, income, and racial characteristics of the population), city size is independently related to total per pupil expenditures. It is also related to teachers'

[23] Robert C. Wood, *1400 Governments* (Garden City, N. Y.: Doubleday Anchor Books, 1961), p. 31.

Table 3-2 Correlations and Path Coefficients
for the Dependent Variable:
General Budget Expenditures

Dependent Variable: General Budget Expenditures

Independent Variable	Zero Order Correlation	Path Coefficient
Catholic population	.610	.922
Index of reform government	−.015	.521
Community poverty	−.100	.422
Economic diversification	−.045	−.408
Decentralized decision-making structure	.237	.394
Highly educated population	−.057	.382
Population size	.310	.369
Civic voluntary organization activity	.042	−.126
Industrial activity	−.062	.097
Residual	—	.544

NOTE: This table gives the correlation of each variable with general budget expenditures without controlling for other variables ("Zero Order Correlation") and while controlling for them ("Path Coefficient").

SOURCE: Terry N. Clark, "Community Structure, Decision-Making, Budget Expenditures, and Urban Renewal in 51 American Communities," *American Sociological Review* (August 1968), p. 588. Reprinted by permission of the American Sociological Association.

salaries, teacher turnover, and private school enrollment. Political system characteristics, however, are not importantly related to educational policy outcomes. Thus, urban environmental variables—size among them—are more influential in determining educational policy than the structural characteristics of political systems.[24]

Population variables are also important in explaining levels of public service development among eighty-three San Francisco area municipalities. Whether a city is in a retarded, transitional, or advanced stage of policy development is closely related to its population, size, density, and growth—variables that are treated as indicators of challenges (pressures) from the environment. A basic assumption of the

[24] Thomas R. Dye, "Governmental Structure, Urban Environment, and Educational Policy," *Midwest Journal of Political Science* (August 1967), pp. 353–80.

Table 3-3 The Social Character of Cities and Educational Policy Outcomes

Educational Policy Outcomes	Size SIM.	Size PAR.	Education SIM.	Education PAR.	Occupation SIM.	Occupation PAR.	Income SIM.	Income PAR.	Nonwhite SIM.	Nonwhite PAR.	Property SIM.	Property PAR.
Per pupil expenditures	.40*	.41*	−.04	−.13	−.01	−.02	.47*	.30*	−.39*	−.41*	.32*	.34*
Expenditures relative to income	−.14	.07	.15	.07	.14	−.02	−.11	−.06	−.09	−.02	−.39*	−.30*
School tax rate	.03	.04	.22	−.05	.25	.09	.29*	.25*	−.31*	−.16	−.10	−.16
Local school support	.11	.03	.02	.11	−.08	−.17	.34*	.25*	−.17	−.08	.23	.06
Teachers' salaries	.31*	.28*	−.05	−.17	−.02	.00	.42*	.29*	−.30*	−.26*	.19	.11
Teacher turnover	.28*	.17	.15	−.01	.11	.04	.11	.08	−.08	.02	−.05	.14
Teacher-pupil ratio	−.03	−.02	−.07	.02	−.13	−.15	−.01	.11	.24*	.25*	−.02	−.17
Teachers without degrees	.05	−.18	−.45*	−.31*	−.36*	.07	.02	.30*	.05	−.27*	.07	−.06
Teachers with Masters	−.01	.02	.23	.17	.15	−.06	.18	−.02	−.14	−.05	.21	.20
Drop-out rate	−.12	−.05	.35*	.26*	.24*	−.06	.20	.10	−.04	.16	.07	.01
Private school enrollment	.25	−.04	−.45*	−.40*	−.36*	.07	.23	.38*	.07	−.01	.45*	.29*

NOTE: Figures are simple and partial correlation coefficients for sixty-seven cities; partial coefficients show the correlations between policy variables and each environmental variable while controlling for all other environmental and structural variables; an asterisk indicates a significant relationship at the .05 level.

SOURCE: Thomas R. Dye, "Governmental Structure, Urban Environment, and Educational Policy," *Midwest Journal of Political Science* (August 1967), p. 362. Reprinted by permission of the author and Wayne State University Press.

San Francisco study is that demand inputs by groups and voters are closely related to population variables. "For instance, the larger a city's population, the more and the more diverse demands [sic] are likely to be made on policy makers (and moreover, the more and more diverse demands for policies coping with problems stemming from environmental challenges are likely to be made)."[25] The data indicate that the greater a city's size, density, or growth, the more developed its policies. "The data suggest that city councils adopt policies which are congruent with needs rooted in pressures from the environment."[26]

Population density is correlated with total (not per capita) welfare expenditures in 228 cities with 25,000 or more residents. As density of population increases, so does welfare spending. And density is more important in the explanation of welfare spending than low income population.[27] Also, per capita spending for services in 212 metropolitan areas is positively correlated with population size. The data in the metropolitan study pertain to the combined spending of all governmental units in the metropolis.[28]

Twenty years ago Hawley showed that city expenditures in seventy-six communities correlated with their population size and density, thus confirming the belief that spending rises to meet the need for services generated by population growth in the city. More interesting, however, was Hawley's finding that per capita expenditures by city governments were more closely related to the size of the population living *outside the city* than within it. This finding supports in striking fashion the belief that city spending develops in part to meet needs generated by the population living outside the city's boundaries. The latter's activities within the city evidently generate pressures for services that in fact have a greater impact on city spending than the city's own population.[29]

---

[25] Heinz Eulau and Robert Eyestone, "Policy Maps of City Councils and Policy Outcomes: A Developmental Analysis," *American Political Science Review* (March 1968), pp. 125–26.

[26] *Ibid.,* p. 133.

[27] *Froman,* "Public Policies in Cities," p. 107.

[28] Brett W. Hawkins and Thomas R. Dye, "Metropolitan 'Fragmentation': A Research Note," *Midwest Review of Public Administration* (February 1970), pp. 17–24.

[29] Amos H. Hawley, "Metropolitan Population and Municipal Government Ex-

Hawley's analysis suggests an important degree of interdependence between populations living within and outside cities. A more extensive study completed in 1959 suggests the same thing. Surveying 462 cities, Harvey E. Brazer found that "the smaller the proportion of the metropolitan area's population that is accounted for by the central city, the greater are its per capita outlays."[30] This same conclusion turned up in a recent study of 36 metropolitan areas. In addition, the latter study found that the smaller the central city's proportion of the population, the greater the per capita expenditures *for the entire metropolitan area*. However, the authors of this study reject any explanation of this phenomenon that stresses service burdens placed on central cities by suburban populations. They suggest that other characteristics of metropolitan areas having a relatively small proportion of their population in central cities—in particular, size and regional influences—explain the association of central city proportion of metropolitan population to expenditures. "It is in the North, particularly in the Northeast, that central city boundaries have responded least to the outflow of population. The larger areas also tend to contain less of their population in the central cities, and these areas, too, allowing for regional differences, have higher levels of fiscal behavior than the smaller areas."[31]

Despite noteworthy irregularities, then, several studies testify to the importance of population size, density, and proportion in the central city. The significance of these findings lies in what they indicate about pressures from the urban environment, i.e., forces that shape demand inputs. Evidently population size, density, and suburbanization produce pressures for more governmental services—and not simply higher total expenditures but also more expenditures *per capita*. Except for the observation that more people require more services, we have no data to define precisely the link between population variables and demand behaviors; but theory stressing the impact of human differentiation on government is suggestive. The theory holds that population size and

---

penditures in Central Cities," *Journal of Social Issues* (January-March 1951), pp. 100–108.

[30] Harvey E. Brazer, *City Expenditures in the United States* (New York: National Bureau of Economic Research Incorporated, 1959), pp. 66–68.

[31] Alan K. Campbell and Seymour Sacks, *Metropolitan America: Fiscal Patterns and Governmental Systems* (New York: Free Press, 1957), pp. 155–57.

spread imply heterogeneous populations, group competition, and diverse demands.

> Large numbers involve . . . a greater range of individual variation. . . . The personal traits, the occupations, the cultural life, and the ideals of the members of an urban community may, therefore, be expected to range between more widely separated poles than those of rural inhabitants. That such variation should give rise to the spatial segregation of individuals according to color, ethnic heritage, economic and social status, tastes and preferences, may readily be inferred.[32]

It might also be inferred that such variation would give rise to multiple and diverse needs and demands for governmental services. Evidently, urbanization is synonymous not only with increased population heterogeneity but also with increased pressures on government for services.

Class and Economic Resources

It makes sense to argue that the more resources available to cities, the more cities will spend. Cities with a greater proportion of high income citizens, businesses, or industries possess more capacity to tax and hence to spend. On the other hand, cities with more low income residents may experience greater need or demand for public services. Well-to-do people with relatively abundant personal resources are little in need of publicly bestowed goods and services. This line of reasoning suggests that someone must want to spend money in order for it to be spent. Thus, a factor conditioning the relationship of capacity to city spending must be the policy demands, or preferences, of masses, organizations, unofficial elites, and official elites.[33]

Some of the published research indicates an important positive relationship between class, capacity, and spending, while another portion of the literature indicates no important relationship. One recent

---

[32] Louis Wirth, "Urbanism as a Way of Life," in *Louis Wirth: On Cities and Social Life,* ed. Albert J. Reiss, Jr. (Chicago: University of Chicago Press, 1964), p. 70.

[33] Research grounded in this approach is found in Eulau and Eyestone, "Policy Maps of City Councils and Policy Outcomes."

study shows a negative relationship between class and city spending. A few studies show both higher and lower class standing positively correlated with spending. A few show neither. There is, in short, no firm pattern.

Philadelphia area municipalities have policies that reflect the social rank and life style characteristics of their residents. Lower social rank communities (which have fewer resources) spend less for services and maintain lower tax rates. The disparity in spending is most pronounced for schools.[34] Both taxes and spending, however, reflect the preferences—as much as the capacity—of community populations. People of similar social status cluster together residentially and have similar preferences about the goals government ought to serve. Evidently, these preferences are successfully communicated to policy makers in the Philadelphia suburbs.

Status or life style differences are also associated with different policy choices among five Wisconsin central cities and their thirty-eight suburbs. Differences in the social character of city and suburb are related to contrasting policy choices by city and suburban governments, at least in the larger urbanized areas. For example, higher status, family-centered suburbs spend more money per child on education than central cities. However, in smaller urbanized areas, where status differences between cities and suburbs are not as great, there is less differential in educational expenditures, and the cities spend more than the suburbs.[35]

Total general expenditures in thirty-six metropolitan areas are closely related to measures of class (per capita income and percent owner-occupied houses). In addition, the correlation of class with expenditures is positive and significant whether the unit of analysis is central cities, fringes outside central cities, or entire metropolitan areas. Also, income is correlated with taxes regardless of the unit of analysis.[36]

---

[34] Oliver P. Williams *et al., Suburban Differences and Metropolitan Policies: A Philadelphia Story* (Philadelphia: University of Pennsylvania Press, 1965), pp. 221–22.

[35] Thomas R. Dye, "City-Suburban Social Distance and Public Policy," *Social Forces* (September 1965), pp. 100–106.

[36] Campbell and Sacks, *Metropolitan America*, pp. 134–44.

In a study of fifty-one cities indicators of both high and low class standing were found to be related to general expenditures and urban renewal expenditures. Tables 3–1 and 3–2 show that even when the influence of other variables is considered, both "community poverty" and "highly educated population" contribute to the explanation of urban renewal and general expenditures.[37]

Urban school segregation is negatively related to class characteristics of the population in the North and positively related to them in the South. Table 3–4 shows that these findings survive controls for other variables (see the columns marked "partial"). One might expect higher status populations to accept desegregation more readily and in the North increases in adult educational and occupational levels are indeed associated with decreases in pupil and teacher segregation. However, in the South increases in these class characteristics are associated with increases in segregation, even when the influence of other factors is controlled.[38] This correlation may reflect the significant role of the middle class in preserving segregationist values in the South.

Still another study showing the importance of social rank to the explanation of policy is Hawley's study of urban renewal. Hawley's primary interest is the relationship of concentrated community power, in the elitist sense, to urban renewal success. Noting that researchers usually find that managerial and proprietary personnel constitute key power figures, Hawley uses census data on managers, proprietors, and officials to measure concentrated power. The *lower* the ratio of managers, proprietors, and officials to the total employed labor force, the greater the concentration of power. In other words, a situation in which there are few managerial personnel relative to the total labor force indicates concentrated power. The data are derived from ninety-five cities of over 50,000 population that at the end of 1959 had arrived at the execution stage of their urban renewal projects. The evidence shows that the greater the concentration of power, the greater the urban renewal success. Even when the impact of other possible influences is considered—including age of city housing, type of government, size of city manufacturing plant, median income, and education—"power

[37] Clark, "Community Structure in 51 American Communities."
[38] Dye, "Urban School Segregation."

Table 3–4 Environmental Variables and Public School Segregation in Northern and Southern Cities

Segregation Measures

Environmental Variables	Northern Cities NEGRO PUPILS Simple	Northern Cities NEGRO PUPILS Partial	Northern Cities NEGRO TEACHERS Simple	Northern Cities NEGRO TEACHERS Partial	Southern Cities NEGRO PUPILS Simple	Southern Cities NEGRO PUPILS Partial	Southern Cities NEGRO TEACHERS Simple	Southern Cities NEGRO TEACHERS Partial
Negro pupils as percentage of total	.76*	.60*	.79	.67	.46	.66	.35	.36
Status characteristics of city population								
Adult education	−.46*	−.34*	−.51	−.42	.20	.52*	−.03	.63*
White collar employment	−.56*	−.44*	−.57	−.51	.12	.32*	−.08	.58
Family income	−.04	−.25	−.15	−.25	.06	.05	−.10	.29
Status characteristics of Negro population								
Adult education	−.42*	−.20	−.46*	−.12	.05	.11	−.07	.20
White collar employment	−.14	.19	−.13	.27	.33*	.46*	.16	.27
Family income	−.05	.13	−.19	.05	.02	.10	.19	.05
Ethnicity	−.31*	−.21	−.39*	−.39*	−.24	−.40*	−.43*	−.62*
Size of city	.49*	.37*	.43*	.38*	.16	.21	.06	.24
Age of city	.54*	.32*	.53*	.38*	.12	−.11	−.10	−.44*
Private school enrollment	.25	.17	.22	.02	.35	.28	.17	.59

NOTE: Figures are simple and partial correlation coefficients for the relationships between pupil and teacher segregation measures and environmental variables for Northern and Southern cities respectively; partial coefficients show the influence of each environmental variable while controlling for *all* other environmental variables including Negro pupil percentages; an asterisk indicates a significant relationship.

SOURCE: Thomas R. Dye, "Urban School Segregation: A Comparative Analysis," *Urban Affairs Quarterly* (December 1968), p. 158. Reprinted by permission of the author and the publisher, Sage Publications, Inc.

concentration" is consistently associated with urban renewal success.[39]

One of the main determinants of educational expenditures in cities is community wealth. Both median family income and property value per pupil are related to expenditures per pupil.[40] Other class attributes of the urban population correlate with some educational policy outcomes. For example, the higher the educational level of the population, the fewer number of teachers in the school system without degrees. Similarly, the higher the occupational level of the population, the fewer number of teachers without degrees.[41]

Data on all 212 metropolitan areas in 1960 indicate that general per capita expenditures in the metropolis are positively correlated with the income of the metropolitan population. (To a lesser extent, general expenditures are also correlated with occupation and education.) Income, in fact, is more closely related to total per capita expenditures than population size. When specific services are considered, income is correlated with education, police, fire, and library expenditures per capita.[42]

It is also worth noting that both the educational policy study and the metropolitan study reveal that political system variables are less determinative of policy outcomes than environmental variables. And income is the most important environmental variable in both studies.

Median family income is an important explanatory variable in Brazer's study of 462 cities. Per capita expenditures for all services increase as income rises, and the relationship is particularly close for recreation and sanitation expenditures.[43] In all cities of over 25,000 population class measures correlate positively with per capita employ-

[39] Amos H. Hawley, "Community Power and Urban Renewal Success," in *Community Structure and Decision-Making: Comparative Analyses,* ed. Terry N. Clark (San Francisco: Chandler, 1968), pp. 393–405.

[40] Dye, "Governmental Structure, Urban Environment, and Educational Policy," pp. 362–63. See also Werner Z. Hirsch, "Determinants of Public Education Expenditures," *National Tax Journal* (March 1960), pp. 24–40, and Seymour Sacks and William F. Hellmuth, *Financing Government in a Metropolitan Area* (New York: Free Press, 1960).

[41] Dye, "Governmental Structure, Urban Environment, and Educational Policy," pp. 362–65.

[42] Hawkins and Dye, "Metropolitan Governmental 'Fragmentation.' "

[43] Brazer, *City Expenditures in the United States,* pp. 29 and 67.

ment in educational services. Also, lower income correlates with larger expenditures for welfare.[44]

In contrast to the testimony of the studies cited so far, there are other studies indicating that class is not closely related to expenditures. For example, per capita planning expenditures in 190 cities are not correlated with high or low class standing (defined as white collar employees, percentage of incomes over $10,000, percentage of incomes under $3,000).[45] Similarly, total per capita spending in cities over 25,000 is not correlated with income, occupation, poor living conditions, or unemployment.[46] In addition, a study of 37 suburban municipalities in the St. Louis area shows only a weak association between municipal social rank (an indicator of resource capacity) and the policy attitudes of city councilmen.

> Most councilmen, regardless of the social rank of their communities, were in favor of increasing city taxes to provide better city services, annexing surrounding communities, and bringing new industries into their communities. . . . Although there was a slight difference in the relative emphasis in communities of varying social rank, most councilmen who were interviewed reported that their councils emphasized policies which encouraged economic growth and secured greater life amenities.[47]

This finding raises a very important question about the impact of resource capacity on city policies. If resources, an environmental factor, do not shape policy through the intervening attitudes of city councilmen, how do they shape policy?

Another study of resource capacity focuses on eighty-three San Francisco area municipalities. Viewing capacity as a limiting condition shaping city policies, the authors of the study hypothesize that the higher a city's resource capacity (per capita assessed valuation), the more developed its public services are likely to be. However, the data do not support this hypothesis. In fact, more low development cities

[44] Froman, "Public Policies in Cities," pp. 106–107.
[45] Lineberry, "Community Structure and Planning Commitment," Table 1.
[46] Froman, "Public Policies in Cities," p. 106.
[47] Bryan T. Downes, "Municipal Social Rank and the Characteristics of Local Political Leaders," *Midwest Journal of Political Science* (November 1968), p. 534.

have high resource capacity than cities in advanced stages of development. This negative finding about the relationship of resource capacity to policy development may be explained in the following terms. Policy development is dependent on the willingness of policy makers to use resources, and their willingness may depend on the intensity of pressures from the environment, regardless of available resources; when demand inputs are weak or nonexistent, new policy commitments will not be made.[48]

Interestingly, the conclusion of the St. Louis study that city socioeconomic status is unrelated to councilman policy attitudes is supported by the San Francisco data. The policy orientations of San Francisco area councilmen are not related to city resource capability.[49]

One recent study of 200 cities shows a *negative* relationship between standard measures of social class and expenditures. The initial hypothesis is that as the urban population's class standing goes up, so do taxes and expenditures. However, the data strongly reject this hypothesis. All class measures (median family income, white collar occupation, and median school years completed) are negatively related to taxes and expenditures.[50]

Industrialism

A related type of environmental characteristic that evidently generates pressures for public spending is industrialism. Industrialism is seen as a pressure stimulating higher city expenditures and also as a producer of tax resources. The latter suggests that industrial development constitutes an important part of a city's resource capacity.

Evidence on the relationship of industrialism to urban policy outcomes is conflicting. Wood's study of governmental spending in the

---

[48] Eulau and Eyestone, "Policy Maps of City Councils and Policy Outcomes," p. 133.

[49] Robert Eyestone and Heinz Eulau, "City Councils and Policy Outcomes: Developmental Profiles," in *City Politics and Public Policy,* ed. James Q. Wilson (New York: Wiley, 1968), p. 58.

[50] Robert L. Lineberry and Edmund P. Fowler, "Reformism and Public Policies in American Cities," *American Political Science Review* (September 1967), pp. 701–16.

New York metropolitan region indicates that, next to population size, measures of industrialism are most closely related to expenditures. These data confirm "a very common interpretation of the relationship between economic development and local government. A highly industrialized community suggests the presence of business property which, per square foot of land, yields assessed valuations higher than any alternative kind of land use, and these can be readily and lucratively tapped through the existing tax system."[51] In other words, industrial growth generates more resources for government, and it also generates needs that require higher expenditures.[52] Other evidence also reveals the importance of industrialism and manufacturing. For example, in all cities of over 25,000 population general per capita expenditures are positively related to "per capita manufacturing establishments" and also to "per capita manufacturing establishments employing 20 or more persons." Although other factors are more important in the explanation of expenditures, these two variables are among those listed as important by the author. On the other hand, data on 51 cities indicate that industrial activity is of minor importance in explaining either urban renewal or general expenditures.[53] Also, Brazer's study of 462 cities indicates that employment in manufacturing, trade, and services does not contribute materially to differences in per capita expenditures, except when industrial suburbs are compared with residential suburbs. However, per capita city expenditures tend to increase generally as the ratio of employment in manufacturing, trade, and services to population rises.[54]

Race and Ethnicity

Among all community variables studied—including city size and age, ethnicity, and status characteristics of the population—Negro pupils as a percentage of total pupils is the strongest correlate of school segregation both in the North and the South. In fifty-five cities Negro

---

[51] Wood, *1400 Governments,* p. 44.
[52] *Ibid.,* p. 46.
[53] Clark, "Community Structure in 51 American Communities," pp. 587–88.
[54] Brazer, *City Expenditures in the United States,* pp. 30 and 67.

pupil and teacher segregation are more closely correlated with Negro pupil percentages than with any other environmental or system variable. Analysis shows, in addition, that this relationship does not depend on the intervening effect of other variables. Evidently it is much more difficult to adopt an effective desegregation policy in cities with large Negro enrollments.[55] This in turn suggests that the presence of more Negroes leads to less integration, regardless of region.

Also of interest is the *absence* of any strong independent relationship between the status levels of Negro subpopulations and the degree of segregation maintained by city schools. One might expect that well-educated, middle-class Negro subpopulations would be in a better position to reduce segregation. "Moreover, we might expect Negro children from families of higher education, occupation, and income levels to be 'acceptable' to whites and therefore less likely to inspire white resistance to desegregation." However, analysis does not support the generalization that Negro status levels independently assist desegregation.[56]

Several other educational policies—in addition to the extent of segregation—are associated with the percentage of nonwhites in the population. Nonwhite population is negatively related to per pupil expenditures and teachers' salaries. Where the proportion of the nonwhite population is highest, expenditures and salaries are lowest.[57] Also of interest is the fact that nonwhite population is negatively related to education expenditures by metropolitan area governments generally, not just central city governments. In addition, nonwhite population is negatively related to general per capita expenditures in metropolitan areas.[58]

School segregation also correlates with ethnicity (national origin). Contrary to the hypothesized relationship, the existence of large white ethnic subpopulations is associated not with increases, but with decreases, in school segregation (see Table 3–4). Moreover, ethnicity

[55] Dye, "Urban School Segregation."
[56] *Ibid.,* p. 155.
[57] Dye, "Governmental Structure, Urban Environment, and Educational Policy," p. 362.
[58] Hawkins and Dye, "Metropolitan Governmental 'Fragmentation.'"

appears to have an independent (negative) relationship with desegregation even when other variables are controlled. Cities with larger ethnic populations tend to be less segregated.

However, ethnicity is not closely related to civil service coverage, city planning expenditures, or federal urban renewal grants (a measure of a city's commitment to urban renewal) in the 309 cities with 1960 populations of over 50,000. There are, for example, only weak correlations between the percentage of foreign stock and planning expenditures per capita when examined within regions of the country (excluding the South). Interestingly, the observed relationship, though weak, is in a negative direction in the Northeast, indicating that the greater the ethnic population the less the expenditures. This evidence supports the theory that ethnic populations have an orientation toward policy that includes a primary regard for their own advantage and an opposition to expenditures that do not directly benefit their families.[59] However, data on 200 cities over 50,000 directly conflict with the same theory. In this study the degree to which ethnicity is related to policy is examined for general expenditures and taxes, not planning and urban renewal alone. Both taxes and expenditures are *positively* correlated with ethnicity, and they are correlated in both reformed and unreformed cities[60] (see Table 3–5). This finding suggests that, contrary to the earlier cited theory, ethnic populations are generally pro-expenditure and support many public expenditures that do not directly benefit their families. Additional support of this conclusion comes from data on all cities over 25,000 population. A larger per capita expenditure for city government is associated with a higher percentage of foreign born persons.[61] (On the other hand, there is little association between ethnicity and per capita employment in educational services.[62])

---

[59] Raymond E. Wolfinger and John Osgood Field, "Political Ethos and the Structure of City Government," *American Political Science Review* (June 1966), pp. 321–24. Lineberry's data show no relationship between ethnicity and planning expenditures in 190 cities. "Community Structure and Planning Commitment."

[60] Lineberry and Fowler, "Reformism and Public Policies," pp. 713–14.

[61] Froman, "Public Policies in Cities," p. 105.

[62] *Ibid.,* p. 106.

Table 3–5 Correlations Between Ethnicity and Religious Heterogeneity and Outputs in Reformed and Unreformed Cities

Correlations of	*Government Type*			*Election Type*		*Constituency Type*	
	Mayor-Council	Manager	Commission	Partisan	Nonpartisan	Ward	At-large
Taxes with:							
Ethnicity	.49	.26	.57	.61	.43	.56	.40
Private school attendance	.38	.15	.37	.33	.37	.41	.25
Expenditures with:							
Ethnicity	.36	.02	.21	.48	.21	.44	.13
Private school attendance	.34	−.01	.07	.25	.24	.40	.05

SOURCE: Robert L. Lineberry and Edmund P. Fowler, "Reformism and Public Policies in American Cities," *American Political Science Review* (September 1967), p. 713. Reprinted by permission of the American Political Science Association.

Religion

Religious variables also contribute to the explanation of urban policies. According to a recent study of 51 communities, Catholic population, in fact, is more closely associated with urban renewal expenditures and general budgetary expenditures than a whole series of other variables including population size, decentralized decision-making structure, educated population, industrial activity, reformed government, and civic organization activity. The relationship of Catholic population to expenditures is the strongest of any of the factors when the others are taken into account[63] (see Tables 3–1 and 3–2). Evidence supporting the generalization that Catholic population is associated with higher expenditures is also found in a more extensive analysis of 200 of the nation's 309 cities of over 50,000 population. Attendance in private (mainly Catholic) schools is correlated with taxes and ex-

[63] Clark, "Community Structure in 51 American Communities."

penditures (see Table 3–5). The correlation of private school attendance with taxes and spending is higher in unreformed than reformed cities, but it is positive in both. The association of Catholic population with higher city expenditures is consistent with theory stressing the impact of population diversity on policy outcomes. Religious diversity evidently generates pressures for public spending, possibly to seek group advantage or to thwart group disadvantage.

Private school enrollment is also associated with school segregation, according to a recent study of 55 cities. As private school attendance goes up, segregation does likewise (see Table 3–4). Evidently, the removal of white children from public schools makes it more difficult to reduce segregation, even if governmental officials choose to do so.[64] On the other hand, Catholic percentage is not correlated with city planning expenditures, according to an analysis covering 190 communities.[65]

Conclusions

The research covered in this chapter shows that large and dense populations and large minority (racial, religious, and ethnic) subpopulations correlate with general city spending and spending for specific services. These correlations, while not uniform, suggest that larger, denser, and more heterogeneous environments generate demands for services by various segments of the population[66] and that city governments often respond favorably to these demands. More heterogeneity brings increased spending for services that benefit a portion, most, or all of the population. Class characteristics of city populations as well as city resource capacity are not consistently related to policy outcomes, perhaps because the key factor in policy output is actual demand behaviors of population groups, private elites, or officials.

This pattern of findings is consistent with theory stressing the policy relevance of urban heterogeneity, the political impact of membership in groups that are not expressly political, and the relationship

[64] Dye, "Urban School Segregation," p. 157.
[65] Lineberry, "Community Structure and Planning Commitment," p. 728.
[66] See Froman, "Public Policies in Cities," p. 104.

of variations in the environment of urban governments to demand inputs. It is thus consistent with the theme that if one hopes to explain urban policies he must widen his explanatory horizons beyond the political system and study the properties of the community environment and how these relate to the demand inputs communicated to official policy makers.

chapter 4
Community Politics and Urban Policies

In explaining urban policies political scientists have always emphasized behavior within the political system and characteristics of the system. In fact, they have so persistently emphasized political variables that recent research showing the importance of environmental variables has evidently provoked some to try to resurrect system characteristics in policy explanation. To scholars whose training leads them to look first within the system, it may be comforting to find evidence that political forms, policy preferences of officials, and formal political leadership roles (such as the mayor's) affect policy. But whatever else they have done, studies showing the importance of socioeconomic environments in policy explanation have raised serious doubts about the relevance of many variables that political scientists had earlier valued for their ability to explain public policy. The burden of proof has now shifted to those who would maintain that system variables are in themselves sufficient for explaining policy outputs.[1]

Ironically, political science has come almost full circle in its treat-

---

[1] Richard I. Hofferbert, "Elite Influence in Policy Formation: A Model for Comparative Inquiry" (Paper delivered at the 1968 meeting of the American Political Science Association, Washington, D. C.), pp. 2 and 3.

ment of the impact of system properties on city policies. Under the influence of good government presuppositions, political scientists once attributed almost magical qualities to official institutions and leaders—that is, to formal political power. However, community power studies showing the impact of unofficial elites and policy studies showing the impact of socioeconomic environments and deliberate efforts to disperse political power have eliminated most such tendencies. Indeed, they have led to speculation that urban government is weak, in danger of disintegration, and "devoid of most of the properties of a manageable enterprise," to use Robert C. Wood's felicitous phrase. Wood and Edward C. Banfield, among others, suggest that sufficient power to develop and to execute policy can barely be amassed in the nation's cities, even by a tightly organized political organization like the Democratic party in Chicago.[2] Far from being a purposeful, rational, initiative-taking enterprise, urban government is seen as incapable of gathering to itself sufficient power to overcome the city's centrifugal tendencies, disposed to wait for others to take the policy initiative, and capable of exerting little impact on the quality of city life even when it does take action. And when one considers, on top of everything else, growing minority group demands for decentralization and neighborhood autonomy, it is tempting to conclude that the "collapse of the classic model" of the urban political system's importance is complete.

Is the situation really that bad? Does politics make any important difference in city policy output? Do the formal arrangements of government, whenever they were created, function to the advantage of some groups and to the disadvantage of others in the way they structure access to policy influence? Or have political scientists been barking up the wrong tree when they try to explain policy by looking at what happens within the system? Does the policy output of the system respond to environmental stimuli virtually irrespective of the system's structure or process? Or is Robert H. Salisbury correct when he stresses the central role of elected political leadership (specifically, the mayor) in run-

---

[2] Robert C. Wood, "The Contributions of Political Science to Urban Form," in *Urban Life and Form*, ed. Werner Z. Hirsch (New York: Holt, Rinehart & Winston, 1963), pp. 100 and 114, and Edward C. Banfield, *Political Influence* (New York: Free Press, 1961), pp. 236 and 237.

ning the urban policy enterprise? Salisbury does not, it should be understood, suggest that the "new convergence" of political power under the mayor's leadership can solve the great problems dominating the urban agenda. He only stresses the central role that formal political power plays in determining city policies,[3] whatever impact these may have on the quality of urban life.

This chapter explores the evidence of the political system's influence on city policy. The studies described here show that system has a policy impact, but *none of them shows that system variables have a bigger impact than environmental variables.* However, many studies do demonstrate that *system is important to policy explanation simultaneously with environmental factors.* Urban renewal, enforcement of traffic laws, fluoridation, school desegregation, police treatment of juvenile offenders, wage garnishment litigation, stages of policy development, and per capita expenditures for services—all of these are to some degree shaped by system variables.

The importance of system variables also stands out in the pluralist stream of the community power literature.[4] Pluralists find that one type of group wielding power in the community is the one that is supposed to, namely, official governmental actors. In the pluralist literature the political process, especially the interactions and choice-making activities of officials with formally endowed prerogatives,[5] does shape policy. Pluralists thus respond to the argument that dominant power resides outside of government by pointing to evidence that elected officials, administrative experts, and line departments often (1) initiate actions,[6] (2) affect decisions,[7] (3) make decisions in their own auton-

[3] Robert H. Salisbury, "Urban Politics: The New Convergence of Power," *Journal of Politics* (November 1964), pp. 775–97.

[4] The studies cited in this section concern the policy consequences of decentralized, competitive power structures. In other words, power structure is treated as an independent variable (the one doing the explaining).

[5] See Hofferbert, "Elite Influence in Policy Formation," p. 4.

[6] Banfield, *Political Influence,* and Roscoe C. Martin *et al., Decisions in Syracuse* (Garden City, N. Y.: Doubleday Anchor Books, 1965).

[7] M. Kent Jennings, *Community Influentials* (New York: Free Press, 1964), and Martin Meyerson and Edward C. Banfield, *Politics, Planning, and the Public Interest* (New York: Free Press, 1955).

omous areas,[8] and (4) balance political forces and assemble power, thereby overcoming the city's tendencies toward inaction.[9] However, it is important to remember that these same pluralist studies also reveal evidence of "outside" power, often in different policy areas. For example, one study concludes: "Economic leaders . . . tend to dominate in essentially 'private' types of decisions that entail the use of nongovernmental resources. Political leaders generally control what we have called 'public' issues, i.e., those requiring the expenditure of public funds."[10]

Police norms—the expectations of the job—are important in explaining the treatment of juvenile offenders in two cities. Compared to "Eastern City," "Western City" has a "professionalized" police force with more formal training and adherence to impersonal, professional rules. In Western City a juvenile "is one and one-half to two times as likely to come into contact with the police and, once in contact with the police, one and one-half times as likely to be arrested and cited rather than reprimanded."[11] Nor is this difference due to the existence of more crime in Western City; the overall crime rates are comparable. The main factor is the professionalism of the police force in Western City, the fact that it operates on universalistic rules. (Other system properties also seem to be at work. In Eastern City policemen are required to appear if there is a court hearing, thus meaning more work for them if they cite a juvenile. This requirement appears to influence their treatment of juvenile offenders.)

Unfortunately for advocates of system variables in policy explanation, however, the police study indicates that professionalism and nonprofessionalism may have a prior environmental cause. Eastern City's policemen are more working class, ethnic, and inclined to live in multiple housing units than Western City's. A majority of Eastern

---

[8] Wallace S. Sayre and Herbert Kaufman, *Governing New York City* (New York: Norton, 1965, 1960), and Robert Presthus, *Men at the Top* (New York: Oxford University Press, 1964).

[9] Banfield, *Political Influence,* and Robert A. Dahl, *Who Governs?* (New Haven: Yale University Press, 1961).

[10] Presthus, *Men at the Top,* p. 406.

[11] James Q. Wilson, "The Police and the Delinquent in Two Cities," in *City Politics and Public Policy,* ed. James Q. Wilson (New York: Wiley, 1968), p. 181.

City's policemen, moreover, are from Eastern City itself—often from the neighborhoods they patrol. Many have a background that includes membership, as a child, in neighborhood gangs. Eastern City's style of law enforcement against juveniles is consistent with these differences. It is based on personal loyalties, neighborhood interests, and particularistic standards. Evidently, community values influence the behavior of police officers, but with the data available from the two cities the independent impact of community values on juvenile arrest rates cannot be directly measured.

A study of the use of court action to attach debtor's wages in four cities considers system properties and other factors. Socioeconomic differences among the cities do not explain differences in the litigation rate, but another environmental factor is important, namely, shared values concerning the level of governmental activity and the willingness to use official governmental agencies compared with informal, private bargaining. The data indicate that debtor-creditor conflicts are most likely to ripen into litigation where the local political culture places a high value on governmental activity and bureaucratized relationships.[12] Legal structure (pressure from federal bankruptcy officers, state laws on court fees, the presence of a local court) is also a factor, but it is impossible to estimate the effect of legal structure compared with political culture.[13] However, structure does have some effect. On the other hand, commonly emphasized political variables—in particular, partisan politics—are not involved.

School desegregation decisions in eight cities are made by those who are supposed to make them, namely, school boards, and not by outside forces. The personal values of school board members determine the policy outcomes.[14] In addition, appointive boards are less influenced by outside forces and more inclined to look favorably on the goals of the civil rights movement than elected boards. The data indicate no direct influence by extragovernmental elites. But indirectly their influence is felt. Economic notables are influential in the type of school

---

[12] Herbert Jacob, "Wage Garnishment and Bankruptcy Proceedings in Four Wisconsin Cities," in Wilson, *City Politics and Public Policy*, pp. 208–11.

[13] *Ibid.*, p. 212.

[14] Robert L. Crain and James J. Vanecko, "Elite Influence in School Desegregation," in Wilson, *City Politics and Public Policies*, pp. 127–48.

board members recruited, their influence being largely determined by the extent to which they have stayed in the city.

Governmental action, in the form of land use policies, is important in adapting to the forces of urbanization (in sixty-four municipalities in the New York metropolitan area). Land use controls thwart the type of rapid growth that can produce tremendous service pressures on local governments.[15]

Community values, socioeconomic variables, and the values of official political elites have been studied for their effect on public assistance programs (in twenty-nine Massachusetts cities). Intercity differences in the proportion of children receiving Aid to Families with Dependent Children (AFDC) are closely associated with such socioeconomic variables as the percentage of women separated or divorced, the percentage of families with annual incomes under $3,000, and the percentage of nonwhite persons under 18 years of age. The effect of socioeconomic variables on AFDC expenditures is also examined, but in this case with negative or inconclusive results. Differences not explained by these variables suggest that eligibility rules are not uniformly applied by local officials: "The possibility remained that the differences resulted to a significant degree from differences in the welfare agencies' use of discretion."[16] An in-depth analysis of two cities markedly different in expenditure rates established that expenditure differences did in fact reflect differences in the agencies' use of discretion. They were not, however, explainable by differences in community values. Elected local officials consistently expressed open hostility to the AFDC program. The urban-rural character of communities also proved unsatisfactory as an explanation of public assistance differences.

Local AFDC directors, however, differed considerably in their goals and norms. In one city the director emphasized rigid adherence to rules; in another the director was client-oriented and flexible about rules. In the first city rules were interpreted in such a way as to limit

---

[15] Robert C. Wood, *1400 Governments* (Garden City, N. Y.: Doubleday Anchor Books, 1964).

[16] Martha Derthick, "Intercity Differences in Administration of the Public Assistance Program: The Case of Massachusetts," in Wilson, *City Politics and Public Policy,* p. 251.

the exercise of discretion; and in both cities the outcomes were those sought by the director, who enjoyed a high degree of bureaucratic autonomy. "To the extent that discretion is available locally, it belongs to professional administrators, most of all to the one at the head of the agency. It is his values and preferences that are expressed in the local government's application of state laws and rules."[17] Differences in public assistance do not seem to be the result of objective differences among clients so much as different values among official elites.

Fiscal and land use policies in thirty-seven St. Louis area municipalities are partially affected by system variables (councilmen's socioeconomic background characteristics), but community characteristics are also involved. Councilmen of higher socioeconomic status tend to emphasize the council's proposing programs that advance the city's interests, and suburbs with such councilmen tend to tax and to spend more. "However, this explanation for the fiscal policies pursued by communities whose councilmen have higher socioeconomic status is only partial and somewhat inadequate."[18] The data suggest that the community environment—population size, resource capability, and citizens' policy preferences—is more important. Characteristics of the council's decision-making process, policy attitudes, and perceptions of issue conflict—all system properties—are not important in explaining fiscal and land use policies among St. Louis area municipalities.

A study of sixty cities that had one or more urban renewal projects in 1957 shows somewhat later entry, but swifter action, by manager-run as compared with mayor-run cities. This finding is explained in a manner consistent with theory concerning the more politicized nature of mayor-council government. Assuming that manager governments are more inclined to seek consensus (and mayoral governments to accommodate persistent differences about policy) one might expect manager governments to place a higher value on maintaining a sense of agreement—and thus to postpone entry into a controversial undertaking until broad agreement is achieved. "In mayor-council cities, lead-

---

[17] *Ibid.*, p. 257.

[18] Bryan T. Downes, "Suburban Differentiation and Municipal Policy Choices: A Comparative Analysis of Suburban Political Systems," in *Community Structure and Decision-Making: Comparative Analyses,* ed. Terry N. Clark (San Francisco: Chandler, 1968), pp. 243–67.

ers may be more ready to risk opposition, seeing it as inevitable and general consensus as impossible; they may, in fact, place a value on pointing up the disagreements which do exist in order to maintain party discipline, or even to prevent adoption of the council-manager plan."[19] Intensive case studies conducted in twenty of the urban renewal cities indicate slightly greater program achievement in manager-run cities, but this finding is confounded by the consistent effect of population size, an environmental variable. Greater achievement is associated with greater size. The author concludes that, by itself, governmental form is not a decisive factor in urban renewal achievement but that it is nonetheless a factor.[20]

Types or sets of policy outcomes are also associated with system properties. Williams and Adrian find that a city's relative emphasis on (1) promoting economic growth, (2) providing and securing life's amenities, or (3) only maintaining traditional services (caretaker government) depends in part on political system characteristics. Maintaining only traditional services is in conflict with the manager plan, for example, because the manager is a problem-solver by profession. "It is against his professional code of ethics to let the city's physical plant deteriorate for the sake of low taxes. The clash between the manager plan and caretaker government does not stop with professional values, however. Career advancements for managers are based upon concrete achievements, not simply satisfied councilmen."[21] Manager government is conducive to a city's economic growth and to provision of amenities, as is the nonpartisan ballot. However, environmental factors are also involved. Support of economic growth and amenities generally comes from higher income groups, and both policy types are also associated with a high incidence of home-owned industries.

Sets of policy outcomes have also been studied in eighty-seven San Francisco area municipalities. Policy outcomes (in the form of spend-

---

[19] George S. Duggar, "The Relation of Local Government Structure to Urban Renewal," *Law and Contemporary Problems* (Winter 1961), p. 57.
[20] *Ibid.*, p. 62.
[21] Oliver P. Williams and Charles R. Adrian, "Community Types and Policy Differences," in Wilson, *City Politics and Public Policy,* p. 33. Four cities are studied by Williams and Adrian.

ing for planning and services) allow the cities to be classified into three stages of development—retarded, transitional, and advanced. The stage of policy development in which a city finds itself is determined in part by councilmen's perceptions of city problems, policy needs, and community goals.[22] Such perceptions, of course, are internal to the political system. The data show that the more diverse the problems perceived by the council, the more developed city policy is likely to be; and the more agreement on the most visible policy problem, the more developed the city.

However, the San Francisco study also shows environment to be important. Challenges from the environment, indexed in terms of city size, density, and population growth, shape policy development. Greater population size, density, and growth are associated with a developed city policy, thus suggesting that "city councils adopt policies which are congruent with needs rooted in pressures from the environment."[23] Another environmental variable, city resource capacity, is not closely related to stages of policy development, even though other research might lead one to assume that the higher a city's capacity the more developed the policy. The authors of the San Francisco study interpret this negative finding to mean that officials' willingness to use resources (a system property) critically affects the relationship between capacity to develop and actual decisions to develop. No assessment is made of whether system or environmental variables are more important, but the main conclusion of the study is that policy development is influenced by the political process itself, not just by challenges or needs arising in the environment.

Socioeconomic variables and structural characteristics of city governments are the subject of a recent extensive analysis of 200 of the nation's cities over 50,000. The study's central concern is the impact of structures, both reformed and unreformed, on the degree to which city governments respond in their policy outputs to socioeconomic cleavages and particular social groups in the community. The data suggest that reformed cities have gone a long way toward accomplish-

---

[22] Heinz Eulau and Robert Eyestone, "Policy Maps of City Councils and Policy Outcomes: A Developmental Analysis," *American Political Science Review* (March 1968), p. 143.

[23] *Ibid.*, p. 133.

ing the reformist goal "to immunize city governments from 'artificial' social cleavages—race, religion, ethnicity, and so on."[24] The translation of environmental conflicts into policy and the responsiveness of political systems to class, racial, and religious cleavages differ according to political structure. Thus, political institutions seem to play an important role in the political process—"a role substantially independent of a city's demography. . . . Nonpartisan elections, at-large constituencies and manager governments are associated with a lessened responsiveness of cities to the enduring conflicts of political life."[25] As Table 4–1 shows, the strength of the correlation between environment and taxing and spending generally decreases regularly with an increase in reform scores. It is also clear, of course, that environmental variables (ethnic and religious characteristics of the population) are closely related to policy in both reformed and unreformed cities, as Table 3–5, p. 82, showed.

Many political scientists have written about metropolitan governmental fragmentation, but few have attempted to measure systematically its policy consequences. One of the assumptions of the metropolitan reform literature, of course, is that fragmentation adversely affects services. Fragmentation is said to increase the cost and to lower the quantity or quality of services. The present author's data show that when fragmentation is measured on a relative scale (number of governments per capita) a few statistically significant and many negative correlations are associated with spending in 212 metropolitan areas, but the correlations are not large (see Table 4–2). In fact, environmental factors (median family income and percentage of white collar workers, high school graduates, and nonwhites) are more important than indicators of fragmentation, as shown in Table 4–3. The data thus fail to reveal any close relationship between fragmentation and public spending, but they do reveal "a relationship." For some services the policy impact of fragmentation, a system property, is measurable and in the expected direction—negative—indicating that as fragmentation increases spending decreases.

[24] Robert L. Lineberry and Edmund P. Fowler, "Reformism and Public Policies in American Cities," *American Political Science Review* (September 1967), pp. 701–16.
[25] *Ibid.*, p. 715.

Table 4–1 Correlations Between Selected Independent Variables and Output Variables by Four Categories of Reformism

	Reform Scores			
	1	2	3	4
Correlations of	(least reformed)			(most reformed)
Taxes with:				
Ethnicity	.62	.41	.50	.34
Private school attendance	.40	.32	.28	.25
Owner-occupancy	−.70	−.39	−.54	−.44
Median education	−.55	−.27	−.32	−.13
Expenditures with:				
Ethnicity	.51	.27	.41	.05
Private school attendance	.46	.23	.16	.08
Owner-occupancy	−.67	−.30	−.54	−.38
Median education	−.49	−.19	−.38	−.37

SOURCE: Robert L. Lineberry and Edmund P. Fowler, "Reformism and Public Policies in American Cities," *American Political Science Review* (September 1967), p. 714. Reprinted by permission of the American Political Science Association.

A study of community efforts in the promotion of hospital projects in 218 communities reveals that system is a factor in the Southeast. Municipal or county governing bodies are important sources of hospital sponsorship in the Southeast whereas in the Northeast not a single community had a governmental body as a sponsoring group.[26]

Form of government and other system properties are related to fluoridation outcomes in several hundred cities. Fluoridation has a better chance of consideration and adoption in cities having a strong executive (manager and partisan mayor) and a relatively low level of direct citizen participation. Broad popular participation, particularly in the absence of strong executive leadership, spells defeat for fluoridation. Also, the mayor's public endorsement is closely correlated with fluoridation adoption, even when a referendum is held. Another struc-

[26] Paul A. Miller, "The Process of Decision-Making Within the Context of Community Organization," in Clark, *Community Structure and Decision-Making: Comparative Analyses*, pp. 307–18.

Table 4-2 Metropolitan Governmental Fragmentation and Spending for Services (Simple, Partial, and Multiple Coefficients)

Per Capita	School Districts per 100,000 (2) Simple	School Districts per 100,000 (2) Partial r1.2(345)	Municipalities per 100,000 (3) Simple	Municipalities per 100,000 (3) Partial r1.3(245)	Townships per 100,000 (4) Simple	Townships per 100,000 (4) Partial r1.4(235)	Special Districts per 100,000 (5) Simple	Special Districts per 100,000 (5) Partial r1.5(234)	Total Governments per 100,000 (6) Simple	Total Governments per 100,000 (6) Multiple R1.2345
Direct general expenditures	.02	.11	.02	−.22**	−.08	−.05	.05	.20**	−.003	.27**
Education	.10	.16*	.03	−.27***	−.05	−.01	.07	.32***	.16*	.37***
Highways	.20**	.13	.03	−.08	.02	.19**	.12	−.06	.21**	.28***
Welfare	.09	.04	−.06	−.02	−.05	.02	−.05	.15*	.02	.17
Health and hospitals	−.14*	−.02	.12	−.11	−.06	−.10	−.11	.03	−.19**	.22*
Police	−.18**	−.05	−.01	−.07	−.09	−.12	.02	−.05	−.30***	.25**
Fire	−.10	−.006	−.01	−.13	−.05	−.04	.11	.01	−.24***	.18
Sewage	.06	.10	−.002	−.07	−.04	−.03	−.006	−.006	.05	.10
Sanitation	−.24***	−.11	.04	−.01	−.06	−.11	−.07	−.23***	−.36***	.36***
Housing and urban renewal	−.16*	−.08	−.10	−.10	−.11	.01	.05	−.01	−.19**	.19
Libraries	.14*	.19**	−.008	−.10	−.15*	−.09	.04	.06	.06	.20
Financial administration	−.13	−.21**	−.02	−.07	−.14*	−.18**	−.08	.08	.07	.24*
Utilities	−.11	−.006	.13	−.08	−.05	−.17*	−.25***	.18**	−.10	.26**

* Statistically significant at the .05 level.
** Statistically significant at the .01 level.
*** Statistically significant at the .001 level.

Table 4-3 Metropolitan Governmental Fragmentation, Metropolitan Environment, and Spending for Services (Multiple and Multiple Partial Coefficients)

Per Capita	Fragmentation Indicators[a]	Environmental Indicators[b]	Fragmentation Controlling for Environment[c]	Environment Controlling for Fragmentation[d]
Direct general expenditures	.27**	.49***	.38***	.55***
Education	.37***	.52***	.42***	.55***
Highways	(.28)**	.19	(.30)***	.22**
Welfare	.17	.36***	.19**	.37***
Health and hospitals	(.22)*	.21	.17*	.51***
Police	.25**	.55***	.32***	.58***
Fire	.18	.46***	.27***	.50***
Sewage	.10	.36***	.16*	.38***
Sanitation	.36***	.41***	.33***	.40***
Housing and urban renewal	.19	.32***	.33***	.42***
Libraries	.20	.40***	.20**	.40***
Financial administration	.24*	.29***	.27***	.32***
Utilities	.26**	.31***	.25***	.30***

NOTE: Parentheses indicate that the fragmentation coefficient is higher than the comparable environmental coefficient.

[a] This column contains multiple coefficients showing the combined explanatory power of the four fragmentation indicators, which are shown in Table 4-2, numbers 2, 3, 4, and 5.
[b] This column contains multiple coefficients showing the combined explanatory power of the four environmental indicators.
[c] This column shows the total explanatory power of the four fragmentation indicators while controlling for the four environmental indicators.
[d] This column shows the total explanatory power of the four environmental indicators while controlling for the four fragmentation indicators.

* Statistically significant at the .05 level.
** Statistically significant at the .01 level.
*** Statistically significant at the .001 level.

tural variable—partisanship—is also related to fluoridation outcomes. In both mayor-run and manager-run cities partisan (as compared to nonpartisan) electoral systems are marked by the larger proportion of adoptions by the city council.[27]

The enforcement of traffic laws in 508 cities is closely related to at least one system property, namely, the ticketing norms established by senior police officers. "The most important factor affecting a policeman's decision to cite or ignore traffic violators is the demand for tickets by senior officers. Where the incentive system of the department is used to reward active ticket-writers, the police will respond with tickets."[28] Interestingly, the author considers the possibility that departmental norms are the product of general community expectations, or the specific clientele with which traffic police deal. However, correlations of ticketing rates with community income, education, ethnicity, race, and housing characteristics are not high enough to suggest an impact of community expectations or client groups. Of course, the lack of association may only mean that community expectations do not vary systematically with these population characteristics. But the author's conclusion is that something within the political system explains intercity differences in ticketing, namely, the norms (values) of official elites. Court procedures, another system property, are also a factor in ticketing. In many cities the arresting officer must appear in court when the motorist appears. Ticketing rates for these cities are substantially lower than for other cities. In the absence of departmental incentives to write tickets, the author suggests, the requirement of a court appearance discourages policemen from writing tickets.[29]

One environmental variable is found to be moderately associated with ticketing. Cities with less mobile populations have lower rates of ticketing than cities characterized by greater mobility. This finding is explainable in terms of mobility's serving to loosen people's ties to the community, thus making less politically important those characteristics

---

[27] Robert L. Crain and Donald B. Rosenthal, "Structure and Values in Local Political Systems: The Case of Fluoridation Decisions," *Journal of Politics* (February 1966), p. 194.

[28] John A. Gardiner, "Police Enforcement of Traffic Laws: A Comparative Analysis," in Wilson, *City Politics and Public Policies,* pp. 158–59.

[29] *Ibid.,* pp. 161–64.

of the population that would otherwise bring forth political demands. Stable population groupings will likely lead to demands to enforce laws on a personal basis,[30] and unstable populations to demands for "professionalized" enforcement on a relatively impersonal basis. This explanation, the reader will recall, is used by Alford and Scoble to explain the association of high population mobility with manager government.[31]

Conclusions

The studies covered in this chapter do not prove that system variables alone explain policy; on the contrary, most of them show that environmental factors are also important. But the studies do undermine any tendency to explain policy solely as a function of external stimuli should anyone be tempted to do so in the wake of unsuccessful efforts to explain policy solely as a function of internal stimuli. What do these studies show? They show that political leadership roles, perceptions of policy makers, and institutions are factors in urban policy output. They thus suggest that formal political power may be significant—even crucial when other factors are equal—in explaining why some cities spend more and others less, or why some cities create new programs while others do not. Alternatively, these studies suggest that there may be two classes of city policy outputs: those importantly shaped and those only negligibly influenced by political system variables.

The choice-making activities of official elites, the degree to which institutions give differential advantages to specific groups and individuals, the picture of the city and its needs in the minds of official elites —all of these factors have to be taken into account. But the exact weight of system variables in policy explanation cannot be stated until more and better evidence is available. However, it is not misreading the data to note a lack of evidence that system is more weighty a consideration than environment. Unfortunately, many studies reported in

---

[30] *Ibid.*, pp. 168–69.
[31] Robert R. Alford and Harry M. Scoble, "Political and Socioeconomic Characteristics of American Cities," *Municipal Yearbook* (Chicago: International City Managers' Association, 1965).

this and the previous chapter do not really compare the two: they only show that both are "a factor." Studies that do systematically compare environmental and system variables for their impact on policies—such as those by Clark, Downes, Dye, and Hawkins and Dye—show environment to be more important. (Another study, one relating to city planning expenditures, shows neither class of explanatory variables to be important.[32]) It may be symptomatic of the inescapable importance of environmental variables that studies cited in this chapter—and picked to show that *system* is important—show environmental as well as system properties to be associated with the following: police treatment of juvenile offenders, wage garnishment litigation, public assistance, taxing and spending for numerous services, urban renewal, stages of policy development, and the ticketing of traffic violators.

---

[32] Robert L. Lineberry, "Community Structure and Planning Commitment: A Note on the Correlates of Agency Expenditures," *Social Science Quarterly* (December 1969), pp. 723–30.

chapter 5
Extracommunity Influences on Urban Policies

The vertical dimension of community relationships has interested political scientists for many years, but its study is lacking in comparative analysis. Also, a theoretical perspective on vertical ties is generally lacking. Recent developments, however, show promise of comparative research having theoretical underpinnings in a systems model that views the city as involved in two kinds of structured interactions, one horizontal and one vertical. Roland L. Warren, for example, suggests that a distinction should be made between two sets of relationships that community subsystems have.[1] Social, economic, and political subsystems (such as a Masonic Lodge, a local branch of a national manufacturing firm, and a welfare agency) interact with one another in the community—but also with organizations outside the community. These interactions typify, respectively, the community's horizontal and vertical ties.

The wider society, then, is present in the community, and it introduces additional stimuli into community action and policy making. Some of the actions of the local Masonic Lodge, for example, are de-

[1] See Roland L. Warren, *The Community In America* (Chicago: Rand McNally, 1963), especially Chapter 8.

termined from outside by the national organization. Some of the decisions of the local manufacturing plant—to involve itself in a local controversy, for example—are determined at the firm's national headquarters. Some of the policy decisions carried out by the local welfare office are predicated upon state and federal rules. In other words, the local community is to some degree subordinate to the wider society, and so are its institutions. This is not to suggest that community decisions are all made elsewhere or that the city has become wholly a "subordinate polity." But it does suggest that urban polities vary in the degree to which their policy output is shaped by extracommunity influences.

Theory suggests that extracommunity influences affect community decision making by introducing additional resources (such as funds from a national corporation), different criteria for action (such as the goals of the corporation), and more personnel with a wider variety of skills (corporate executives). Extracommunity forces, such as the coming of new industries and federal programs, also affect policy by generating new social or political groupings with distinct goals for government. These components of extracommunity influence lead to a more competitive local power structure (unless, of course, the vertical force is so strong that it takes over completely) and to sociopolitical diversification. Extracommunity influences are, in short, a type of change in the environment of urban political systems that encourages greater diversity in local political interests and demands over policy. Theory on extracommunity influences is thus consistent with other theory emphasizing the policy relevance of socioeconomic heterogeneity.

This chapter is concerned with the relationship of extracommunity influences to city policies. Two sets of vertical ties are covered: political ties with higher levels of government and socioeconomic ties with private organizations.

Political Ties

Untold volumes have been written about the relationship between local government and higher levels of government. Descriptions of state and federal grants to localities and the laws governing their use are plentiful. Also, there is some literature that attempts to assess the impact of

Extracommunity Influences on Urban Policies

federal and state grants on localities and of state laws on urban governmental structure. But none of this research is guided by a theoretical perspective, and almost none of it involves the systematic comparison of one community with another. Nor are most of the studies quantitative in nature. Instead, they contain descriptions of this type: "Federal requirements for an adequate geographic area of jurisdiction promote area-wide planning and administration in some cases but not in a majority."[2]

In some studies only legal provisions are discussed under the heading of "impact" or "effect." For example, a study of the "effects of the war on poverty on local government" describes the law permitting use of private as opposed to public community action agencies, reasons for this law, administrative regulations, and evidence showing that private agencies predominate over governmental ones.[3] The war on poverty is also the subject of Daniel P. Moynihan's *Maximum Feasible Misunderstanding.*[4] Moynihan generalizes broadly about the pattern of community action programs as follows:

> Over and over again, the attempt by official and quasi-official agencies (such as the Ford Foundation) to organize poor communities led first to the radicalization of the middle-class persons who began the effort; next to a certain amount of stirring among the poor, but accompanied by heightened racial antagonism *on the part of the poor* if they happen to be black; next to retaliation from the larger white community; whereupon it would emerge that the community action agency, which had talked so much, been so much in the headlines, promised so much in the way of change in the fundamentals of things, was powerless.[5]

---

[2] "Impact of Federal Urban Development Programs on Local Government Organizations and Planning," prepared for the Committee on Government Operations of the United States Senate by the Advisory Commission on Inter-Governmental Relations (Washington, D.C.: Government Printing Office, 1964), p. 22.

[3] Advisory Commission on Inter-Governmental Relations, *Inter-Governmental Relations in the Poverty Program* (Washington, D.C.: Government Printing Office, April 1966), pp. 23–28.

[4] Daniel P. Moynihan, *Maximum Feasible Misunderstanding: Community Action in the War on Poverty* (New York: Free Press, 1969).

[5] *Ibid.*, pp. 134 and 135. Emphasis in the original.

One impact of the war on poverty, in other words, was to arouse the antagonism of the larger community and its power structure against community action agencies.

On the other hand, there is some evidence that federally sponsored poverty programs have had a beneficial impact on their clientele. An Atlanta study of the impact of community action programs on clients' social position and feelings of alienation indicates a favorable impact. Before-after comparisons indicate that after contact with community action programs the social position of clients was higher and their alienation lower. Not only was total alienation lower after contact, but there was also a lessening of the various dimensions of alienation, such as "powerlessness," "normlessness," and "social isolation."[6]

Still another broad descriptive finding is that federal urban renewal and highway programs cause the displacement of local persons and businesses.[7]

Several studies indicate that certain programs exist in cities because the federal government has put forth all or most of the money to provide for those programs. Federal action, for example, is a major factor in mass transportation policies in Baltimore and Seattle.[8] Also, community mental health centers are being established because of the Mental Retardation Facilities and Community Mental Health Centers Construction Act of 1963. The 1963 Act authorizes grants to states for construction of "Comprehensive Community Mental Health Centers," and several cities have begun to establish such centers under its provisions.[9]

If one backs up a step and asks what factors explain federal action

---

[6] John Dabney Hutcheson, "Social Position, Alienation and the Impact of the War on Poverty" (Ph.D. dissertation, Department of Political Science, University of Georgia, 1969), pp. 67–70.

[7] Advisory Commission on Inter-Governmental Relations, *Relocation: Unequal Treatment of People in Business Displaced by Governments* (Washington, D.C.: Government Printing Office, January 1965). See also Herbert J. Gans, *The Urban Villagers* (New York: Free Press, 1962).

[8] Frank C. Colcord, Jr., "Decision-Making and Transportation Policy: A Comparative Analysis," *Southwestern Social Science Quarterly* (December 1967), pp. 383–97.

[9] See Robert H. Connery *et al.*, *The Politics of Mental Health* (New York: Columbia University Press, 1968).

on urban problems, he finds that "actions within the political system" is the answer suggested by the literature. Actions by official political actors (e.g., Congressmen or Senators), interest groups, and professional experts are emphasized in explaining federal action on urban problems.[10]

In contrast to descriptive, nontheoretical studies, a few studies have appeared that explicitly make use of the dependent polity concept and/or use comparative, quantitative methods in the analysis of vertical political ties. One study having such a theoretical framework is *Small Town in Mass Society*.[11] It is explicitly a study of social life in a community that lacks the power to control fully the institutions that shape its existence, and of the way the community adjusts to forces from outside. Among the outside forces mentioned are "institutional linkages to state and national politics." Under this heading the impact of state subsidies in defining the goals of village government is discussed, the relationships between state and local electoral politics are explored, and federal agricultural policies are described in terms of their impact on the agricultural sector of each community.

A comparative analysis of the impact of higher level governments on local policy is found in Robert C. Wood's *1400 Governments*.[12] Wood notes that, by turning to federal and state governments, sixty-four New York area localities are able to supplement local resources and thus to expand their spending for services. "For the Region as a whole, outside financial assistance is now second only to the property tax as a source of revenue. For several services, [it is] the prime support. In schools, welfare, health, highways, and redevelopment, outside contributions typically outweigh total local contributions for the respective services."[13] Thus, outside support is an important factor in explaining the spending activities of New York area governments. However, Wood also notes the limitations of outside financial

---

[10] *Ibid.*, and Frederick N. Cleaveland, "Congress and Urban Problems: Legislating for Urban Areas," *Journal of Politics* (May 1966), pp. 289–307.

[11] Arthur J. Vidich and Joseph Bensman, *Small Town in Mass Society* (Garden City, N. Y.: Doubleday Anchor Books, 1960).

[12] Robert C. Wood, *1400 Governments* (Garden City, N. Y.: Doubleday Anchor Books, 1961).

[13] *Ibid.*, p. 87.

resources in controlling economic and population forces that bear on the region's government. Grants-in-aid from higher levels of government, while adding to the local budget, do not substantially affect the forces of urbanization.[14]

In a study of taxing and spending in thirty-six metropolitan areas state aid per capita is positively related to per capita general expenditures by central cities, suburban communities, and all SMSA governments combined. Similarly, state education aid per capita positively correlates with per capita education expenditures by central cities, suburbs, and all SMSA governments. A positive relationship between grants from higher levels of government and expenditures by urban governments is also indicated by a study of 462 cities having 1950 populations in excess of 25,000. This study shows that intergovernmental revenue per capita is consistently and positively related to per capita city expenditures.[15] State aid is also related to taxing; that is, per capita taxes by central cities, fringes, and all metropolitan area governments combined are negatively related to per capita state aid. This finding suggests that where local resources produce insufficient tax revenue, state aid compensates; conversely, where there are greater local tax resources, state aid is accordingly lower.[16]

Socioeconomic Ties

As the relationship of the community to the larger society changes, the characteristics of community groupings and the structure of community power undergo change as well. One outside force that affects the local power structure is the coming of new industries to the community. When new industries arrive, they affect local leadership processes by bringing a new set of potential leaders, new resources that can be translated into political influence, and new goals and values. Research from many communities suggests that the coming of absentee-owned

---

[14] *Ibid.*, p. 122.
[15] Harvey E. Brazer, *City Expenditures in the United States* (New York: National Bureau of Economic Research Incorporated, 1959), p. 67.
[16] Allen K. Campbell and Seymour Sacks, *Metropolitan America* (New York: Free Press, 1967), pp. 134–43.

corporations changes the power status quo by fragmenting it in the direction of greater competitiveness or factionalism. However, one also finds the opposite theme in the literature: that corporate executives are as "elephants among chickens" and become an economic ruling class when they move into a local community.[17] This theme is less common than the former, however. Still another theme is that communities dominated by absentee-owned enterprises have lower levels of private and public welfare expenditures than communities in which business enterprises are locally owned. On the other hand, a study in the late fifties found exactly the opposite correlation.[18]

Thus, there are conflicting generalizations about the relationship of absentee ownership to community action. A study of a rapidly growing Southern city in the middle fifties showed that "community projects are usually doomed if they lack the approval of the industrial, absentee-owned corporations." Although the executives constitute no single united clique, "absentee-owned corporations are a decisive force in the power structure of Bigtown, since they constitute a balance of power among the competing interest groups of the community."[19] This conclusion suggests not greater power diversity but concentration as a consequence of the injection of absentee-owned corporations. Moreover, the policy leadership of absentee corporation executives is motivated by corporate, not community, goals.

A strikingly different finding emerges from a study of "Cibola," a Midwestern industrial community of about twenty thousand persons. The Cibola study focuses on historical change in leadership structure. Its main hypothesis is that as an initially self-contained community

[17] Scott Greer, *The Emerging City* (New York: Free Press, 1962), pp. 153 and 154.
[18] See Peter H. Rossi and Robert Crain, "The NORC Permanent Community Sample," *Public Opinion Quarterly* (Summer 1968), pp. 270–71. The relevant studies are C. Wright Mills and Melvin Ulmer, *Small Business and Civic Welfare: Senate Document No. 135,* 79th Congress, 2nd sess. (Washington, D. C.: Government Printing Office, 1946), and Irvin A. Fowler, "Local Industrial Structure, Economic Power and Community Welfare," *Social Problems* (Summer 1958), pp. 41–51.
[19] Rowland J. Pellegrin and Charles H. Coates, "Absentee-Owned Corporations and Community Power Structure," *American Journal of Sociology* (March 1956), pp. 413–19.

develops progressively more ties to the larger society, its pyramid-like, centralized leadership structure becomes increasingly decentralized and competitive. More specifically, the hypothesis is that in the self-contained community those persons exercising major control over the community's economic system tend also to exercise preponderant influence over its political system. As the relationship of the community to the larger society changes, however, the local power structure "bifurcates," in effect divorcing economic from political power. The evidence indicates that in fact "there has been a progressive withdrawal of the economic dominants from active and overt participation in public life in Cibola." As the period of local capitalism passed, the new economic dominants, representing absentee-owned corporations, were increasingly influenced by extracommunity organizations and goals. In other words, the withdrawal of economic dominants is primarily due to the changing relationship of the community's economic system to that of the larger society. Increasingly the executives of Cibola's absentee-owned corporations have adopted a hands-off attitude toward local political decisions.[20]

Support of the generalization that economic-political power becomes bifurcated over time is provided by a study of "Wheelsburg," a town of about 100,000 persons sixty miles from Cibola. In fact, the decline in the proportion of economic dominants holding public office is sharper in Wheelsburg than in Cibola. However, the Wheelsburg study does not support the generalization that absentee-ownership accounts for economic dominants' withdrawal from *public office*. But their withdrawal from *civic leadership positions* does seem to be associated with the introduction of absentee-owned plants. Also of interest in the Wheelsburg study is the fact that on eleven community issues economic dominants (including some representing absentee-owned corporations) either initiated or coinitiated programs of action for six of the eight issues in which they were involved. This finding, of course, suggests that economic dominants have not withdrawn from community decision making, and it contrasts with the Cibola finding in which analysis of two issues showed that the economic dominants were wholly uninvolved. Still, the main conclusion of the Wheelsburg study is that

[20] Robert O. Schulze, "The Role of Economic Dominants in Community Power Structure," *American Sociological Review* (February 1958), pp. 3–5.

political and economic structures that were once inseparable have tended to become bifurcated over time.[21]

A recent study of a Midwestern town of about 10,000 persons also supports the theory that absentee ownership has a pluralizing effect. In "Cornucopia" the establishment of a boat manufacturing plant produced striking effects on the local decision-making process. The new leaders (executives) were specialized on the issues in which they participated, and many of them confined their activities to a single issue. This pattern of behavior was in striking contrast to the traditional leadership structure of Cornucopia. Before the introduction of the factory, 60 percent of the local leaders participated in more than one issue, whereas after its inception only 10 percent participated in more than one issue. This change suggests that the introduction of the factory promoted pluralism and tended to fragment the existing, generalized decision-making structure of the community. This fragmentation of community leadership is an important finding that is consistent with theory suggesting the pluralizing influence of growing vertical ties.[22]

The impact of defense contracting on community leadership has been studied in two communities in Southern California. The study concludes that the injection of defense contracting causes changes in the composition, size, and turnover rate of leadership structures. When one of the communities became intensely involved in defense contracting, its leaders were unable or unwilling to handle the new issues that arose; consequently, they were soon replaced, or the existing leadership structure was expanded to accommodate the new issues. The result was the same in either case—a change in the composition of the leadership.[23]

The generalization that executives of absentee-owned corpora-

[21] Donald A. Clelland and William H. Form, "Economic Dominants and Community Power: A Comparative Analysis," *American Journal of Sociology* (March 1964), pp. 511–21.

[22] Robert Mills French, "The Effect of an Absentee-Owned Industry on Community Decision-Making: The Impact of the Chrome Boat Corporation on Cornucopia's Decisions" (Paper delivered at the annual meeting of the Southern Sociological Association, New Orleans, 1969).

[23] Phillip Edward Present, "Defense Contracting and Community Leadership: A Comparative Analysis," *Southwestern Social Science Quarterly* (December 1967), pp. 399–410.

tions play major roles in community decision making is not supported by research on two upstate New York communities. In neither town do corporation executives of nationally owned plants play preeminent roles.[24] In general, however, this study finds that community decision making is affected by higher levels of government and industry. "In this way the periphery of local autonomy is becoming more restricted." Of interest also is the conclusion that wider political participation, both in the local power structure and in the community at large, is associated with the use of local resources in decisions. "External" resource use is associated with *less* participation both in the general community and in the power structure. This finding suggests the opposite of the theories emphasized in this chapter. The upstate New York study suggests that extracommunity forces produce not pluralism but elitism. A decline, not an expansion, of pluralism is associated with increasing ties between the community and larger social, political, and economic systems.[25]

On the other hand, support of existing theory is offered by a study of four communities, two on the West Coast and two in the South. This study concludes that if the major economic units in the community are home-owned the community power structure is likely to be more centralized.[26] This finding supports the theory that the injection of an outside economic force leads to fragmentation of the existing, relatively homogeneous, power structure.

The only extensive comparative analysis (using forty-one communities) of the relationship between absentee-owned businesses and community influence structure supports the theory that the introduction of organizations with vertical ties brings new resources and sanctions to the local community and these circumstances are conducive to the emergence of competing power structures. Table 5–1 shows that the absence of absentee-ownership of business is associated with a centralized, "pyramidal" power structure and its presence is associated with a more competitive power structure.[27]

---

[24] Robert Presthus, *Men at the Top* (New York: Oxford University Press, 1964), p. 419.

[25] *Ibid.*, p. 432.

[26] Robert E. Agger, Daniel Goldrich, and Bert E. Swanson, *The Rulers and the Ruled* (New York: Wiley, 1964), p. 680.

[27] John Walton, "The Vertical Axis of Community Organization and the Struc-

Table 5-1 Absentee Ownership and Community Power Structure[a]

	Pyramidal Structure	Factional, Coalitional, or Amorphous Structure	Total
Owner[b]			
Present	2	18	20
Absent	12	9	21
Total	14	27	41

NOTE: The cell entries in the table represent communities, rather than studies, since a single study often dealt with two or more towns.

[a] The variable power structure was originally coded in terms of four categories. The categories are collapsed here to avoid small subtotals and to provide a contrast between more and less concentrated power arrangements.

[b] The number of communities in each of these subtables vary because the studies coded do not provide uniform data on each variable.

SOURCE: John Walton, "The Vertical Axis of Community Organization and the Structure of Power" *(Southwestern) Social Science Quarterly* (December 1967), p. 355. Reprinted by permission of *Social Science Quarterly*.

Conclusions

Growing extracommunity ties tend to diversify urban interests, groups, and power structures. Relatively homogeneous populations and leadership structures become, with sufficient vertical ties, relatively heterogeneous. Competition increases. Greater conflict over policy making is a natural consequence of these developments. These are the generalizations that emerge from patterns in the literature on extracommunity variables and city policies. They are consistent with theory that we have earlier encountered stressing the political impact of socioeconomic heterogeneity. It appears that more extracommunity ties generate demands on government from a greater variety of sources and make power structures more competitive. Furthermore, one must anticipate that in the foreseeable future urban communities will have progressively more extracommunity ties. Absentee-ownership is more likely to increase than to decrease; economic interdependence among neighboring communities is likely to increase.[28] Individuals' organizational ties with social, political, and economic institutions beyond their own locality are likely to increase. If the existing literature and theoretical perspectives are any guide, one can anticipate that future analysis will show greater demands on government and more pluralistic power structures developing from these stimuli. Decentralization or deconcentration of political power—and greater demands for services by various population groupings—can be expected.

---

[28] Donald J. Bogue, *The Structure of the Metropolitan Community* (Ann Arbor: Horace H. Rackham School of Graduate Studies, University of Michigan, 1949).

chapter 6
In Perspective

What does the research on urban policy tell us about relationships between urban environments, political systems, and policy outputs? In pursuing this question here we must place our greatest emphasis on patterns in the research literature and our greatest reliance on extensive comparative studies. Our objective is to put the research findings in a theoretical perspective. In spite of weaknesses in the literature, and conflicting evidence as well, it is important, even at this early stage, to get a broad perspective on city policy explanation. A broad perspective is presented here in the form of statements about concepts, such as environmental heterogeneity, system, and policy output. We do not make statements about observables, such as non-white population, that stand antecedent to city expenditures.

Analyses based on data describing urban environments as well as city governments suggest that consideration of urban environments will have to be a prominent feature of any explanatory theory. Under good government presuppositions, of course, the role of the urban environment in shaping public services was largely ignored. However, political scientists no longer attempt to explain policy by means of system variables alone. Recent evidence reveals that city environments—especially the diversity of their populations—are important influences on policy.

Socioeconomic heterogeneity is a factor greatly influencing the structural characteristics of city political systems and their policy output. For example, greater heterogeneity correlates with the retention of politicized institutions and less heterogeneity with the adoption of reformed institutions. These findings suggest that socioeconomic heterogeneity indexes competing political interests and that the more numerous the competing interests the more potent the demand inputs for retaining politicized institutions adept at accommodating differences over the services government has to bestow, and at responding to group demands. In addition, heterogeneity correlates with spending for services; evidently, the more segmentalized the urban population, the more numerous the demands for services. The main point is that heterogeneity gives rise to multiple needs and demands for public services; when these demands are transmitted to government or felt by government officials with sufficient force, government responds.

We can summarize current findings on urban policy explanation in the following schema. The first model in Figure 6–1 states that the impact of socioeconomic heterogeneity is not materially affected by any intervening variable. In this situation system properties do not importantly affect policy; a higher level of heterogeneity is in itself sufficient to spur increased output or to generate policies more responsive to the needs or demands of the population. From the literature that finds environment to be important, and especially the literature that compares environment and system as explanatory concepts, we conclude that this model explains more of the variation in policy output than alternative models.

The second model in Figure 6–1 states that the effects of socioeconomic heterogeneity are filtered through and altered by intervening political system characteristics (a, a'), and that the system affects output independently of the environment (b) to some degree. It suggests that we cannot ignore the way political structures and processes affect access and condition influence from the community, or beyond it. Evidently a high level of socioeconomic heterogeneity encourages the retention of politicized, responsive, group-accommodating institutions and influences other system properties (e.g., a greater sensitivity to problems on the part of official policy makers) that in turn promote a higher level of expenditures and affect the distribution of policy benefits. Evidently some system properties that affect policy are not importantly affected by environmental forces, and some are. From the research covered in

Figure 6–1   Summary Models Ranked According to
Explanatory Importance

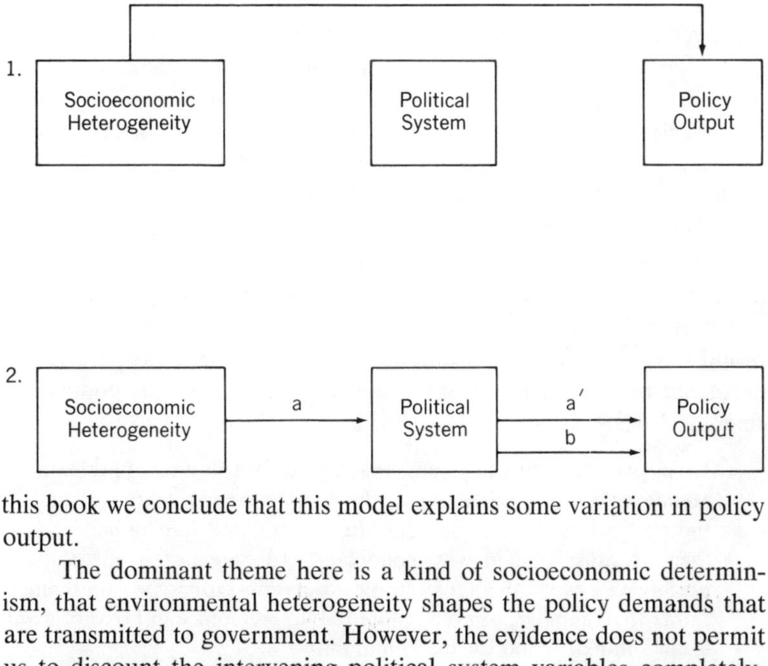

1. Socioeconomic Heterogeneity → Policy Output; Political System (not connected)

2. Socioeconomic Heterogeneity —a→ Political System —a′, b→ Policy Output

this book we conclude that this model explains some variation in policy output.

The dominant theme here is a kind of socioeconomic determinism, that environmental heterogeneity shapes the policy demands that are transmitted to government. However, the evidence does not permit us to discount the intervening political system variables completely. Recent critiques of the literature suggest that greater attention should be given to measuring the independent effect of the calculations of officials as well as other attributes of the decision-making process. To do this, it is argued, more refined political variables tapping the dynamics of the decision-making process must be developed and used.[1] So should more refined methods, such as computer simulation of the

---

[1] Richard I. Hofferbert, "Elite Influence in Policy Formation: A Model for Comparative Inquiry" (Paper delivered at the 1968 meeting of the American Political Science Association, Washington, D. C.); Bryan T. Downes and Timothy M. Hennessey, "Theory and Concept Formation in the Comparative Study of Urban Politics: Problems of Process and Change" (Paper delivered at the 1969 meeting of the American Political Science Association, New York City); and James W. Clarke, "Environment, Process and Policy: A Reconsideration," *American Political Science Review* (December 1969), pp. 1172–82. See also John P. Crecine, *Governmental Problem Solving* (Chicago: Rand McNally, 1969), for evidence of the importance of internal decision rules.

policy process. It remains to be seen, of course, whether better system measures or methods will produce results very different from those thus far obtained. If they do not, presumably the simpler approaches will be preferred under the rule of parsimony. (It is also interesting to speculate on the possible results using better measures of environment.) However, it does seem likely that different models may explain different policies and that subtheories as special cases of broader theory can be developed.[2] On the other hand, these embellishments of theory might well confirm or only slightly modify earlier conclusions regarding the relative importance of environmental and system factors.

We should note, in any case, that the discovery of an even closer correlation between socioeconomic variables and policy output than that presently perceived would not constitute sufficient explanation. It would only give rise to the question, To what extent have we really *explained* public policy by observing its association with population characteristics?[3]

> Unless we are willing to assume that a given distribution of preferences among voters that arises out of the socioeconomic characteristics of those voters is directly and faithfully translated into public policy, then we must explain why politicians and bureaucrats chose some preferences over others, or impute to certain groups one preference rather than another, or even ignore public preference in favor of what leaders think is good for the community.[4]

The way in which urban heterogeneity correlates with actual demand behavior has not been determined. This deficiency is crucial because it means that we cannot really estimate the validity of commonly used indicators of policy-relevant demand inputs. To what degree does

---

[2] This is the conclusion for the analysis of state policies in Charles F. Cnudde and Donald J. McCrone, "Party Competition and Welfare Policies in the American States," *American Political Science Review* (September 1969), pp. 858–66. See also Ira Sharkansky and Richard I. Hofferbert, "Dimensions of State Politics, Economics, and Public Policy," in the same issue of the *American Political Science Review,* and Robert E. Crew, "Dimensions of Public Policy: A Factor Analysis of State Expenditures," *Social Science Quarterly* (September 1969), pp. 381–88.

[3] James Q. Wilson, ed., *City Politics and Public Policy* (New York: Wiley, 1968).

[4] *Ibid.*, p. 5.

population heterogeneity really indicate either policy conflict or demands on city government (whether public- or private-regarding, for example)?[5] We do not know how well the proportion that a group's membership bears to the city's total population predicts that group's impact on government—nor can we even discern the group's preferences independent of their impact! Should that proportion prove to be a poor predictor of the group's demands, impact, or preferences, much of the research based on theories about the political relevance of broad social groups would be ravaged.

What research does indicate, however, is that heterogeneity makes a difference in urban policy outputs. From evidence that heterogeneity correlates with policy, researchers infer that diversity-generated demands are transmitted to the political system and have an effect.[6] But the way in which this sequence works is a matter to be illuminated by further research.

Of course, political scientists have already begun to devise constructs describing how environmental heterogeneity can shape demands. For example, one model of the relationship (or "linkage") between mass preferences and government decisions suggests that political parties "aggregate" individual preferences and transmit them to the political system as demands. Interest groups are said to do the same thing. A second model of linkage suggests that government decision makers often have the same preferences as their constituents. According to this conception, mass preferences are represented directly in the kinds of people elected to office. The main idea here is that elected officials can be expected to have preferences fairly typical of their constituents or else they would never have been nominated or elected in the first place. Still another model of linkage suggests that government policy makers act not from their own preferences but from their perceptions of mass preferences, whether these coincide with their own

---

[5] See Downes and Hennessey, "Theory and Concept Formation," Part 1, p. 14.
[6] For more direct evidence that citizens' pressure has a positive effect on city services, see James J. Vanecko, "Community Mobilization and Institutional Change: The Influence of the Community Action Program in Large Cities," *Social Science Quarterly* (December 1969), pp. 609–30. Effective citizen pressure seems partly a function of action agency emphasis on community mobilization as well as an already existing high level of citizen participation.

views or not. Policy makers bow to the masses' wishes either because they are obsessed with the norm that a legislator should mirror his constituents' views faithfully or because they are convinced that doing so is the best way to stay in office, or both.

Still another model asserts that government policy makers do what they themselves want to do (i.e., pursue their own policy preferences) in relative freedom from any concern about demands or pressures from the masses. The idea is that in addition to "inputs" from outside there are important "withinputs" from inside that influence system output. In other words, policy makers often direct demand activities at one another, occasionally going first to the people to build support. When the latter happens, "demand inputs" become difficult to distinguish from "demand withinputs," and studying the initiation and weight of policy-relevant interactions becomes a complex research problem. Interestingly, the "withinputs" model has recently received support from a study of political representation in San Francisco area municipalities. Of the 82 councils studied, "as many as 36 did not in any discernible manner seem to act in response to any politically organized view in the public. These 36 councils seemed to rely on their own sense of what the community needs were."[7] In addition, the same research project found that city councils not responsive to community interests or groups are seldom removed from office.[8] This conclusion suggests that councils may be unresponsive to the preferences of the electorate and still not be turned out of office.

In any case, a critical question remaining in the analysis of urban policy is the specification of linkages that account for observed correlations between socioeconomic environments, systems, and policies. To understand these linkages, political behavior (i.e., participation) directed at the scope of government (i.e., policy) must be studied in greater detail. Even though socioeconomic diversity seems to be an important influence on policy, an ever-present, necessary, interven-

---

[7] Kenneth Prewitt and Heinz Eulau, "Political Matrix and Political Representation: Prolegomenon to a New Departure from an Old Problem," *American Political Science Review* (June 1969), p. 429.

[8] *Ibid.*, p. 433.

[9] Robert E. Agger, Daniel Goldrich, Bert E. Swanson, *The Rulers and the Ruled* (New York: Wiley, 1964), p. 40.

ing variable between social or economic variables and policy is somebody's political participation.[9] The actual political behavior of masses, groups, associations, and official and unofficial elites must become a prime focus of research. Politically active persons and groups will have to be analyzed and answers sought to such questions as who initiates contacts, how patterned they are, and what their content is.

This does not mean that the study of heterogeneous population groupings should be abandoned. On the contrary, environments can be treated as prior to and influencing group political values and behaviors. Group life can thus be seen as an important mediator between city environment and policy output.[10] An important key to understanding demand behavior, moreover, may be the attachments of individuals to groups. For instance, group-differentiated attachments to public officials may influence mass support of officially sponsored policies, such as fluoridation.[11] "Attachments," in turn may be shaped by community size, growth rate, ethnic and racial composition, and occupational and power structures.[12] It may be productive, therefore, to conceptualize the city dweller as an aggregate of attachments to population groups, organizations, and persons. These attachments can then be seen as having environmental antecedents and as shaping the course and outcome of conflicts over policy.[13] In the larger, more diverse city there are, it is reasonable to assume, more numerous (and conflicting) attachments relevant to policy.

It is worth mentioning, finally, that urban policy findings—including those stressing environmental influences—have important practical implications as well as implications for science. Reliable general knowledge about the forces that shape urban policies can be used to bring about wanted changes. With rigorously acquired knowledge about the interconnectedness of urban phenomena intervention can be made

[10] See, for example, Robert Eyestone and Heinz Eulau, "City Councils and Policy Outcomes: Developmental Profiles," in Wilson, *City Politics and Public Policy,* pp. 47 and 48.

[11] This is the conclusion in Maurice Pinard, "Structural Attachments and Political Support in Urban Politics: The Case of Fluoridation Referendums," *American Journal of Sociology* (March 1963), pp. 513–26.

[12] Pinard, "Structural Attachments and Political Support."

[13] James S. Coleman, *Community Conflict* (New York: Free Press, 1957).

effective. Understanding the independent impact of various forces is predictively useful and tells us where best to intervene. Without such knowledge intervention can bring about unintended consequences. It may do more harm than good. Obviously, the interventionist implications of findings about the importance of socioeconomic environments sharply conflict with "good government" strategies. Recent research suggests that if one wants to improve governmental output the way to do it is to deal with the environment at least as much as with the system. Indeed, not intervention within the system but outside it is indicated. Intervention might better be aimed at the urban environment than at formal government. For example, from the fact that urban public services are influenced by economic levels in the community it follows that a logical strategy for improving services would be to seek the reduction of poverty, unemployment, low wage employment, and racial and class discrimination in education and jobs. Perhaps the best reform strategy is to move against imperfectly functioning socioeconomic mobility mechanisms, not against governmental forms.

Findings about the importance of socioeconomic heterogeneity have other practical implications as well. Greater heterogeneity means not only increased pressures on government for services but also strains on government's conflict-managing capacity. The bigger and more diverse the urban population, the greater the difficulty of reaching public decisions that satisfy important groups. Also, the more diversity, the greater the difficulty of providing wanted goods and services in such quantities that mass—or even group—support of the system is maintained. There is, in short, an increased danger of disaffection and alienation from an urban political system subjected to the strains of high population heterogeneity. Indeed, at some level of heterogeneity the urban governmental machinery may become literally unmanageable. Hopefully, that forbidding threshold has not yet been reached in any city.

Index

Absentee ownership, community power and, 106–11
Administration, government
 environmental correlates of, 15–17, 19–41
 political correlates of, 41–55
Adrian, Charles R., 63n, 92
Advisory Commission on Intergovernmental Relations, 55
Agger, Robert E., 29n, 64, 110n, 118n
Aid, government, 102–3, 106
Aid to families with Dependent Children (AFDC), 90
Alford, Robert R., 20n, 21, 23n, 26n, 27n, 28n, 29n, 30n, 32n, 34–35, 39n, 41n, 42n, 50, 56, 99
Annexation, governmental, 44, 48, 49, 51
At-large election districts, 19
 environmental correlates of
  ethnicity, 22–23, 26
  population, 34
  religion, 38
 political correlates of, 41–42, 94
Attachments, community, 119
Antiurbanism, 3–4
Autonomy, local, 16

Banfield, Edward C., 86, 87n, 88n
Barth, Ernest A. T., 63n
Belknap, George, 63n
Bensman, Joseph, 105n
Blacks, segregation of, 75, 79–80, 113. *See also* Segregation
Bogue, Donald, J., 112n
Booth, David A., 53n, 63n
Bray, Robert L., 56n
Brazer, Harvey E., 71, 76, 79n, 106n

Campbell, Allen K., 71n, 106n
Catholic population
 class and, 28
 governmental forms and, 38, 39
 manufacturing and, 39
Cibola study, 107–8
Cities
 administration—environmental characteristics of 15–17, 19–41
 characteristics of, 5–6
 developmental stages of, 93
 extracommunity forces and, 13
 systems analysis of, 11–18
 types of, 30
Citizen participation, 45, 117–19
City-county consolidation, 44

121

City manager governments
  environmental correlates of, 5, 8
    class, 29
    economic base, 30
    ethnicity, 21–23, 26
  political correlates of, 41–42
Clark, Terry N., 28*n*, 66*n*, 79*n*, 82*n*, 91*n*, 120
Clarke, James W., 29*n*, 52*n*, 115*n*
Class
  city expenditures and, 72–78, 83
  economic base and, 30–32, 72–74
  education and, 74
  governmental forms and, 17, 20, 28–30, 43, 59
  housing and, 28, 29
  income and, 28
  occupation and, 28, 29
  population mobility and, 35
Clelland, Donald A., 109*n*
Cnudde, Charles F., 116*n*
Coates, Charles H., 107*n*
Colcord, Frank C., Jr., 104*n*
Coleman, James S., 119*n*
Combination election districts, 19
Commissions, governmental administration, 19
  class and, 28–29
  ethnicity and, 22–23
  population and, 36
  suburbs and, 34
Community, size of, 119
  fragmentation and, 45
  governmental forms and, 32–35
  policy impact of, 17
  spending and, 65–72
Community environment, characteristics of, 15, 17, 18, 57
  class, 28–32, 35, 43, 59–78, 83
  economic base, 30–32, 59
  elites, 62–65
  ethnicity, 21–27, 35, 39–40, 80–82
  population, 32–36, 65–72
  region, 38–41
  religion, 35–38, 39, 43, 55, 59, 82
  school segregation, 75, 80–81, 83
Community politics
  roles in, 86–87
  system variables of, 87–100
    debts, 89

Community politics—*Cont.*
  system variables of—*Cont.*
    environment, 91, 93
    land use, 90, 92
    outcomes, 92
    police norms, 88–89
    population, 91
    resource capability, 91
    school desegregation, 89–90
    traffic enforcement, 98–99
    values, 90–91
Community power studies, 8
Comparative studies, value of, 5–6, 8
Conflicts, indicators of, 8–9
Connery, Robert H., 104*n*
Consolidation, 49
  city-county, 19
  intermunicipal, 44
Cooperation, intermunicipal, 50–52
Cornucopia study, 109
Corporations, absentee-owned, community action and, 106–9, 111
Cosmopolitan attitudes, political integration and, 52–55
Council government administration
  abandonment of, 56*n*
  environmental correlates of
    class, 28
    economic base, 30–31
    ethnicity, 21–23, 26
    race, 26
  political correlates of, 42
Councils
  community and, 118
  as governmental form, 10
Crain, Robert L., 89*n*, 98*n*, 107*n*
Crecine, John P., 115*n*
Crew, Robert E., 116*n*
Cutright, Phillips, 30, 31*n*, 38*n*, 42–44, 50

Dahl, Robert A., 88*n*
D'Antonio, William V., 64*n*
Decentralized government, 44–47, 55, 86, 112
Defense contracting, 109
Democratic party, 86
Demographic studies. *See* Population
Dentler, Robert A., 63*n*

Index

Derthick, Martha, 90n
Deutsch, Carl, 51n
Dewey, John, 4
Districts, election
 at-large, 22–23, 26, 34, 38, 41, 42, 94
 ward, 19, 22–23, 26, 42
Diversity, political success and, 49–51, 57–58
Downes, Bryan T., 58n, 77n, 91n, 100, 115n, 117n
Duggar, George S., 92n
Dye, Thomas R., v, 5n, 44n, 47–51, 52n, 54, 61n, 66n, 68n, 70n, 75, 76n, 80n, 83n, 100

Economic base governmental forms and, 30–32, 59
Economics
 elite power and, 63–64
 expenditures and, 72–78
 governmental structure and, 56
Education, 5
 class and, 74
 ethnicity and, 81
 expenditures for, 67, 69, 76–77
 governmental forms and, 28, 29, 48
 segregation and, 75, 79–81
Election districts
 ethnicity and, 22–23, 26
 population and, 34
 regions and, 39
 religion and, 38
 types of, 19
Electoral systems, 117
 environmental correlates of
  class, 28–31
  economic base, 30–32
  ethnicity, 23, 25
  population, 34
  race, 26
  religion, 38
 political correlates of, 41
 types of, 19
Elites
 community, 62–65
 governmental forms and, 59
 school desegregation and, 89–90
Environment
 community, characteristics of, 15, 17, 18, 21–41, 57, 61–84, 87–100

Environment—*Cont.*
 determinants of, 8
  systems analysis and, 13
  variation in, 10
 extracommunity
  influences, 101–12
  variables, 15–18, 41–55, 64–65
 heterogeneity of, 115
Erikson, Eugene C., 64n
Ethnicity, 81, 119
 city output and, 82
 governmental forms and, 10, 21–27, 55, 59
 policy impact of, 17
 population mobility and, 35
 regions and, 39–40
 segregation and, 80–81
 social heterogeneity and, 21, 23
Eulau, Heinz, 70n, 72n, 78n, 93n, 118n, 119n
Expenditures
 class, capacity and, 72–73
 ethnicity and, 81
 federal, 106
 fragmentation and, 94, 96
 industrialism and, 78–79
 life styles and, 73
 manufacturing and, 79
 population and, 65–72
 religion and, 82
 welfare, 70, 77, 107
Extracommunity environment
 influences of, 101–2
  leadership, 109
  political, 102–6
  socioeconomic, 106–12
 characteristics of, 15–18, 41–55, 64–65
Eyestone, Robert, 70n, 72n, 78n, 93n, 119n

Federal government, programs of, 102–6
Federal grants, extracommunity influences of, 102–3
Field, John Osgood, 20n, 26, 27n, 29n, 38, 39n, 40, 42n, 81n
Floro, George K., 10n, 29n
Fluoridation, 5, 10, 119
 city management and, 95, 98

Foreign stock, definition of, 21
Form, William H., 109n
Fowler, Edmund P., 23, 25n, 29n, 32n, 34n, 40n, 57n, 78n, 81n, 94n
Fowler, Irvin A., 107n
Fragmentation
  consequences of, 94
  industry and, 107, 109
  political, 44–47, 55
  spending and, 96–97
French, Robert Mills, 109n
Friedrich, Carl J., 20n
Froman, Louis A., 66n, 70n, 77n, 81n, 83n

Gamson, William A., 65n
Gans, Herbert J., 104n
Gardiner, John A., 98n
Gilbert, Claire W., 62n
Goldrich, Daniel, 29n, 64, 110n, 118n
Gordon, Daniel N., 10n, 21n, 39
Government, 50–51
  aid from, 102–3, 106
  citizen participation and, 45
  consolidation of, 44
  decentralized, 44–47, 55, 86, 112
  federal, programs of, 102–6
  forms of, *see specific forms*
  "good," 6–7
  group representation and, 20
  immigrant influence on, 21–23
  population diversity and, 20
  characteristics of
    environmental, 15, 17, 19–41
    political, 41–55, 57
Grants, extracommunity influence of, 102–3, 106
Greer, Scott, 53n, 107n
Group representation, unreformed governments and, 20

Hanson, Robert C., 63n
Harris, Seymour E., 20n
Hawkins, Brett W., 42n, 44n, 49, 51, 53n, 54n, 70n, 76n, 80n, 100
Hawley, Amos H., 70–71, 74, 76n
Heinz, John P., 10n
Hellmuth, William F., 76n
Hennessey, Timothy M., 58n, 115n, 117n

Heterogeneity, socioeconomic, importance of, 114–20
Hirsch, Werner, 2, 4n, 76n
Hofferbert, Richard I., 17n, 61n, 85n, 87n, 115n, 116n
Holden, Matthew, Jr., 16n
Housing, class and, 28, 29
Hunter, Floyd, 62
Hutcheson, John Dabney, 104n

Immigrants, influence of, 21–23
Income
  class and, 28
  policy studies and, 9
  spending and, 76–77
Industrial cities, governmental form of, 30–32
Industrialism
  effects of, 106–11
  expenditures and, 78–79
Inputs, system analysis, 13
Institutional changes, policy and, 9–10
Institutions, governmental
  environmental correlates of, 15–17, 19–41, 49–51, 59
  political correlates, 41–55, 57–58
  types of, 19–20
Integration
  political, 47–55
  school, 74
Integrative governments, types of, 19
Intellectuals, cities and, 3–4
Intermunicipal consolidation, 44
Intermunicipal cooperation, voting and, 50–52

Jacob, Herbert, 89n
Jefferson, Thomas, 4
Jennings, M. Kent, 63n, 87n
Johnson, Stuart D., 63n
Juvenile offenders, police norms and, 88–89, 100

Kaufman, Herbert, 88n
Kessel, John H., 19n, 20n, 23n, 27, 30, 32n, 33n, 34n, 50

Labor, foreign born, 24–25
Land use policies, 90, 92

Index

Larson, Calvin, 4n
Leaders, governmental policy and, 62–65
Leadership, community, 109
Liebman, Charles, 32n, 56
Life styles
 policy studies and, 9
 political integration and, 54–55
 spending and, 73
Lineberry, Robert L., 23, 25n, 29n, 32n, 34n, 40n, 57n, 66n, 77n, 78n, 81n, 83n, 94n, 100n
Long, Norton, 20n

McCrone, Donald J., 116n
McDill, Edward L., 52n
Madison, James, 56
Manager-council governmental administration
 abandonment of, 56n
 environmental correlates of, 19
  class, 28–29
  economic base, 31–32
  ethnicity, 22–23, 26
  population, 32–33, 35, 36
  race, 26
  region, 38
  suburbs, 34
 political correlates of, 41–43
  communities, 91–92
  integration, 48, 51
Manufacturing
 city expenditures and, 79
 foreign-born employment in, 24–25
 levels of, 39
Manufacturing cities, governmental forms of, 30–32
Martin, Roscoe C., 87n
Marx, Karl, 56
Masotti, Louis, 4n
Mayor-council governmental administration, 19, 86–87
 environmental correlates of
  class, 28–29
  ethnicity, 22–23, 26
  population, 32–33, 36
  regions, 38–40
  suburbs, 34
 political correlates of, 42
  community, 91–92

Metropolitan special district government, 19, 44
Meyerson, Martin, 87n
Miller, Delbert C., 63n
Miller, Paul A., 65n, 95n
Mills, C. Wright, 107n
Minorities, 10, 83
Mobility. *See* Population, mobility of
Moynihan, Daniel P., 103

Negroes. *See* Blacks
Nonpartisan electoral systems
 environmental correlates of, 19
  class, 30–31
  ethnicity, 22–23, 25, 26
  population, 34
  race, 26
  religion, 38
 political correlates of, 41–44
  community, 92, 94

Occupations
 class and, 28, 29
 governmental forms and, 37
Output, systems analysis, 13

Partisan electoral system, 19
 class and, 28–31
 economic base and, 30–32
 ethnicity and, 23–25
 race and, 26
 religion and, 38, 39
Pellegrin, Rowland J., 107n
Pinard, Maurice, 119n
Pluralists, community politics and, 87–88
Police norms
 professionalism and, 88–89, 100
 ticketing and, 98–99
Policy
 outcomes, 15, 17
 output of, 86
 roles in, 86–92
 study of, 8–10
Political systems, characteristics of, 15, 17
Population
 composition of
  city expenditures and, 65–72
  class and, 28

Population—*Cont.*
 composition of—*Cont.*
  governmental form and, 26–27, 32–36
  interdependence and, 71
 diversity of
  government and, 20, 55, 70
  importance of, 113–15, 117
 mobility of
  governmental form and, 32, 35–37
  ticketing and, 98–99
Power structure, community, 101–12
Present, Phillip Edward, 109n
Presthus, Robert, 63–64, 88n, 110n
Prewitt, Kenneth, 118n
Private schools
 expenditures and, 82–83
 governmental forms and, 36–38
 regionalism and, 39
 segregation in, 83
 taxes and, 82–83
Professionalized governments, 20
 class and, 28
 ethnicity and, 21
 religion and, 35–38
Public assistance, community values and, 90–91
Public services, resource capacity and, 77–78
Public spending, 5

Race
 governmental institutions and, 26, 119
 policy studies and, 9
Racial segregation, population size and, 66
Referenda, reorganization, 53n
Reformed governmental institutions, 19–20, 58
 city output and, 82–83
 environmental correlates of
  class, 28–29
  ethnicity, 22–23, 26
  population, 32–34
 policy and, 94–95
 political correlates of, 42, 55, 94
 integration, 49
Reformers, 6–7
Regionalism, governmental form and, 27n, 38–41

Reiss, Albert J., Jr., 7n
Religion
 city output and, 82
 competition and, 43
 governmental forms and, 35–39, 55, 59
 policy impact of, 17
 population mobility and, 35
Republican party, elections and, 43, 51–52
Residence, policy studies and, 9
Retail cities, governmental forms of, 30
Ridley, Jeanne Claire, 52n
Romani, John, 53n
Rosenthal, Donald B., 98n
Rossi, Peter H., 9n, 63n, 107n
Royce, Josiah, 4

Sacks, Seymour, 71n, 76n, 106n
Salisbury, Robert H., 10n, 86–87
Sanders, Irwin T., 11n
Santayana, George, 4
Sayre, Wallace S., 88n
Schmandt, Henry J., 51
Schmuckler, Ralph, 63n
Schnore, Leo F., 26n, 27n, 29n, 34n, 39n, 42n, 50
Schools
 expenditures for, 67–69
 political cooperation and, 50
 private
  expenditures and, 82–83
  governmental forms and, 36–38
  regionalism and, 39
  segregation in, 83
  taxes and, 82–83
 segregation in, 75, 79–80
  community politics and, 89–90
Schulze, Robert O., 108n
Scoble, Harry M., 20n, 21, 23n, 30n, 34, 35n, 39n, 41n, 56, 99
Segregation, racial
 class and, 74
 environmental correlates of, 75
 ethnicity and, 80–81
 population size and, 66
 private schools and, 83
 status and, 80
Sharkansky, Ira, 116n
Sherbenou, Edgar L., 29n

Index

Size, community, 119
  fragmentation and, 45
  governmental form and, 32–35
  policy impact of, 17
  spending and, 65–72
Social determinism, 57
Social heterogeneity, theory of
  ethnicity and, 21, 23
  politics and, 56
  population and, 32
Social rank. *See* Status
Socioeconomic factors, 26n, 56–57
  importance of, 114
  influence of, 106–11
  systems analysis and, 13
Spending. *See* Expenditures
Spill-over, theory of, 51
State aid, 106
Status
  desegregation and, 80
  education and, 74
  elite power and, 64
  political integration and, 48
  spending and, 73
  urban renewal and, 74
  voting and, 50n
Stone, Edwin O., 10n, 29n
Structural policy outcomes, 10
Subsystems
  definition of, 16n
  influence of, 101–2
Suburban communities, 51, 71
  antiurbanism of, 4
  governmental forms of
    class and, 29
    ethnicity and, 25–26
    political integration and, 48–49
    population and, 32–35
    race and, 26
    regional variations and, 39
Swanson, Bert E., 29n, 64, 110n, 118n
System variables, community politics and, 87–100
Systems analysis, data and, 10–18

Taxes
  city output and, 82n
  ethnicity and, 81
  expenditures and, 78
  federal, 106
  population and, 65–66

Teune, Henry, 50n
Traffic laws, enforcement of, 98–99

Ulmer, Melvin, 107n
Unreformed governmental institutions, 19–20, 58
  city output and, 82–83
  environmental correlates of
    class, 29
    ethnicity, 21–27
    population, 32–34
  political correlates of integration, 49
Urban heterogeneity, impact of, 83–84
Urban renewal, 5
  class and, 74
  community politics and, 91–92
  elite power and, 63
  expenditures for, 67
  federal, 104
  influence of, 16

Vanecko, James J., 89n, 117n
Variables, systems analysis and, 13–18
Vidich, Arthur J., 105n
Voting, status and, 50

Wages, garnishment of, 89, 100
Walton, John, 62n, 110n
Ward election districts, 19
  ethnicity and, 22–23, 26
  political correlates of, 42
War on Poverty, 104
Warren, Roland L., 11n, 16n, 101
Watson, Richard, 53n
Wealth, community expenditures and, 76–77
Welfare, 5
  community values and, 90–91
  expenditures for, 70, 77, 107
Wheelsburg study, 108–9
White, Morton, 3n
White collar occupations, 37
Williams, Oliver P., 92
Wilson, James Q., 88n–90n, 98n, 116n
Wirth, Louis, 72n
Wolfinger, Raymond E., 20n, 26, 27n, 29n, 39–40, 42n, 81n
Wood, Robert C., 4n, 7n, 67n, 78, 86, 90n, 105

Young, Roland, 9n

WITHDRAWN
St. Scholastica Library
Duluth, Minnesota 55811